UML DEMYSTIFIED

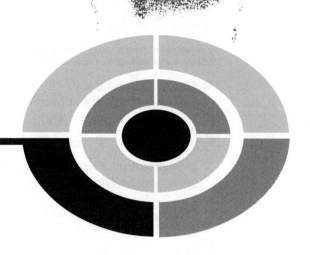

UML DEMYSTIFIED

PAUL KIMMEL

McGraw-Hill/Osborne

New York   Chicago   San Francisco   Lisbon   London
Madrid   Mexico City   Milan   New Delhi   San Juan
Seoul   Singapore   Sydney   Toronto

The McGraw·Hill Companies

McGraw-Hill/Osborne
2100 Powell Street, 10th Floor
Emeryville, California 94608
U.S.A.

To arrange bulk purchase discounts for sales promotions, premiums, or fund-raisers, please contact **McGraw-Hill**/Osborne at the above address.

UML Demystified

234567890 DOC DOC 019876

ISBN 0-07-226182-X

Acquisitions Editor
Wendy Rinaldi

Project Editor
Samik Roy Chowdhury (Sam)

Acquisitions Coordinator
Alex McDonald

Technical Editor
Eric F. Cotter

Copy Editor
James K. Madru

Proofreader
Chris Andreasen

Indexer
WordCo Indexing Services

Composition
International Typesetting
and Composition

Illustration
International Typesetting
and Composition

Cover Series Design
Margaret Webster-Shapiro

Cover Illustration
Lance Lekander

This book was composed with Adobe® InDesign® CS Mac.

In loving memory of my sister Jennifer Anne
who was given just 35 years.

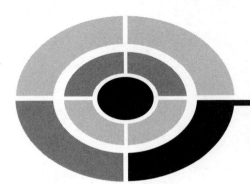

ABOUT THE AUTHOR

Paul Kimmel is the Chief Architect and a founder of Software Conceptions, Inc. He has been designing and implementing object-oriented software since 1990 and has more than a dozen years of experience with modeling languages and was an early adopter of the Unified Modeling Language. Paul has helped design and implement solutions using the UML for some of the largest corporations in the world from international banks, multinational telecommunications companies, logistics and shipping companies, Department of Defense agencies and national and international governmental groups.

CONTENTS AT A GLANCE

CONTENTS

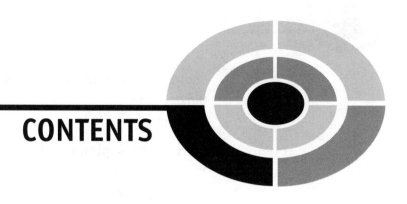

ACKNOWLEDGMENTS

Well into my second decade of writing I have Wendy Rinaldi at McGraw-Hill/Osborne, along with Alexander McDonald and my agent David Fugate at Waterside to thank for this opportunity to write what I believe you will find an informative, entertaining, and easy to follow book on the Unified Modeling Language.

I also want to thank my friend Eric Cotter from Portland, Oregon, for offering to provide technical editing for UML DeMystified. Eric did an excellent job of finding my mistakes, omissions, and in improving the explanations.

Thank you to my hosts at the Ministry of Transportation Ontario in St. Catharines, Ontario. Collaborating with you on CIMS was an enjoyable process and exploring my models and designs with you provided excellent fodder for this book. Thank you Novica Kovacevic, Jennifer Fang, Rod, Marco Sanchez, Chris Chartrand, Sergey Khudoyarov, Dalibor Skacic, Michael Lam, Howard Bertrand, and David He from Microsoft. It was a pleasure working with and learning from all of you.

In 2004, along with Bill Maas, Paul Emery, Sainney Drammeh, Bunmi Akinyemichu, and Ryan Doom, the Greater Lansing area .NET Users Group (glugnet .org) was formed, and I'd like to say hello to all of the great glugnet members and supporters. We meet the third Thursday of every month at 6:00 P.M. on the beautiful campus of Michigan State University. Thanks to MSU for permitting to use their excellent facilities in the Engineering Building and Anthony Hall.

While working in Ontario my sustenance was graciously provided for at Prudhommes in Vineland, Ontario, at exit 55 and 57 and the Honest Lawyer in St. Catharines, Ontario, Canada. Thanks to Lis, Jen Cheriton, Everett, Kathryn, and Kim for food and adult beverage, and the staff of the Honest Lawyer for the wireless access.

Last but not least, I owe a gratitude of debt to my wife Lori and four children, Trevor, Douglas, Alex, and Noah, playing the role of biggest fans and supporters. A family is the greatest blessing. (I would also like to introduce the newest member of our family Leda, an energetic chocolate lab, who waits patiently at my feet as a subtle reminder to push back from the computer and go do something else every once in a while.)

INTRODUCTION

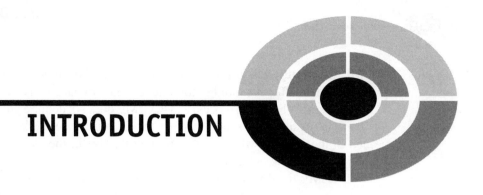

New inventions often occur out of necessity and are documented on napkins long before, if ever, an authoritative and formal definition is provided. The Unified Modeling Language (UML) is just such an example. Individual aspects of what ultimately became the UML were defined by Ivar Jacobson, James Rumbaugh, and Grady Booch out of necessity long before their individual contributions were consolidated into a single definition.

There is a mixed problem with formal and standard specifications. Generally, for an august body of scientists to ratify something it is to be unambiguously and rigorously defined. If you look up the definition of the UML, you will find meta-models that describe to minute detail what is and what is not the UML. The effect is much like reading congressional reports: long-winded, dry, tedious, and with an occasional juicy tidbit. Think of formal definitions versus practical applications like this: there are specific rigorous rules that define something as simple as algebra, but you don't need to know them even though we perform or rely on simple algebra in everyday tasks such as pumping gas. For example, *price per gallon multiplied by number of gallons = total price*. With simple text-to-character substitution we can create arithmetic equations, $p * g = t$, that start to look like those confusing equations from school but make it notationally convenient to determine any quantity of the equation. What I mean is that even people that would identify themselves as math challenged perform math everyday for practical purposes without ever thinking of it what they are doing as solving math problems.

That's the objective behind this book. There are formal and rigorous definitions of the UML and they exist for good reason, but you don't have to know them to use the UML in a practical way. UML linguists have to know the UML intimately to rigorously define just like English professors know grammar intimately to teach it, but you don't have to be an English teacher to communicate effectively. This is true of the UML too; you don't have to know every detail about the UML to use it effectively.

UML DeMystified is written in simple prose and designed to make the UML practical and an effective tool for communicating software analysis and design.

There are many books on process and the UML does not define a process. However, this book is organized in such a manner that if you create the kinds of models as needed in the order in which they appear in this book, then you have a practical beginning of a usable process.

UML DeMystified is a modest-sized book but it is a compilation of more than a dozen years of practical experience working with some of the largest and best known companies in the world as well as many well-known smaller companies, and the UML described in this book is pragmatic, practical, and applicable whether you are building small, medium, or very large applications. In short, UML DeMystified leaves the ivory tower fluff and rigor to other texts and tells you what you need to know to successfully use the UML to describe software.

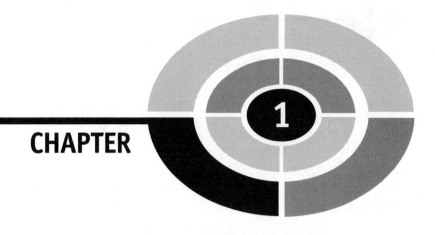

A Picture Is Worth a Thousand Lines of Code

Pictures of little stick people represent the oldest recorded form of communication in human history. Some of these cave art have been dated to be as old as 75,000 years. Oddly enough, here we are at the turn of the twenty-first modern century, and we are still using little stick figures to convey information. That's right, a little stick man we'll call Esaw is a central character in one of the newest languages developed by humans (Figure 1-1).

Esaw

Figure 1-1   Esaw, who is referred to as an actor in the UML.

The language I am talking about is called the *Unified Modeling Language*, or UML. The UML is a language just as sure as, Pascal, C# (C sharp), German, English, and Latin are languages. And the UML is probably one of the newest languages invented by humankind, invented around 1997.

As with other languages, the UML was invented out of necessity. Moreover, as with many languages, the UML uses symbols to convey meaning. However, unlike organic languages such as English or German that evolve over time from common use and adaptation, the UML was invented by scientists, which unfortunately is a problem. Scientists are very smart, but they often are not very good at explaining things to those less scientific. This is where I come in.

In this chapter we will look at the origin and evolution of the UML. We also will talk about how to create pictures using the UML, how many and what types of pictures to create, what those pictures should convey, and most important, when to stop drawing pictures and start writing code.

Understanding Models

A *model* is a collection of pictures and text that represent something—for our purposes, software. (Models do not have to represent software, but we will narrow our scope to software models.) A model is to software what a blueprint is to a house.

Models are valuable for many specific reasons. Models are valuable because they consist of pictures to a large extent, and even simple pictures can convey more information than a lot of text, e.g., code. This is consistent with the somewhat modified old adage that a picture speaks a thousand lines of code. Models are valuable because it is easier to draw some simple pictures than it is to write code or even text that describes the same thing. Models are valuable because it is cheaper, faster, and it is easier to change models than it is to change code. The simple truth is that cheap, fast, easy, and flexible are what you want when you are solving problems.

Unfortunately, if everyone uses different pictures to mean the same thing, then the pictures add to the confusion rather than mitigate it. This is where the UML comes in.

Understanding the UML

The UML is an official definition of a pictoral language where there are common symbols and relationships that have one common meaning. If every participant speaks UML, then the pictures mean the same thing to everyone looking at those pictures. Learning the UML, therefore, is essential to being able to use pictures to cheaply, flexibly, and quickly experiment with solutions.

It is important to reiterate here that it is faster, cheaper, and easier to solve problems with pictures than with code. The only barrier to benefiting from modeling is learning the language of modeling.

The UML is a language just like English or Afrikaans is a language. The UML comprises symbols and a grammar that defines how those symbols can be used. Learn the symbols and grammar, and your pictures will be understandable by everyone else who recognizes those symbols and knows the grammar.

Why the UML, though? You could use any symbols and rules to create your own modeling language, but the trick would be to get others to use it too. If your aspirations are to invent a better modeling language, then it isn't up to me to stop you. You should know that the UML is considered a standard and that what the UML is and isn't is defined by a consortium of companies that make up the Object Management Group (OMG). The UML specification is defined and published by the OMG at *www.omg.org*.

The Evolution of Software Design

If you feel that you are late to the UML party, don't fret—you are actually an early arrival. The truth is that the UML is late to the software development party. I work all over North America and talk with a lot of people at lots of very big software companies, and the UML and modeling are just starting to catch on. This is best exemplified by Bill Gates' own words after his famous "think week" in 2004, where Gates is reported to have talked about the increasing importance of formal analysis and design (read UML) in the future. This sentiment is also supported by Microsoft's very recent purchase of Visio, which includes UML modeling capabilities.

The UML represents a formalization of analysis and design, and formalization always seems to arrive last. Consider car makers in the last century. Around the turn of the last century, every buggy maker in Flint, Michigan, was turning horse carriages into motorized carriages, i.e., cars. This occurred long before great universities such as Michigan State University (MSU) were turning out mechanical engineers trained to build cars and software tools such as computer-aided design (CAD) programs that are especially good at drawing complex items such as car parts. The evolution of formalized automobile engineering is consistent with the evolution of formalized software engineering.

About 5000 years ago, the Chinese created one of the first computers, the abacus. About 150 years ago, Charles Babbage invented a mechanical computing machine. In 1940, Alan Turing defined the Turing computing machine and Presper Eckert and John Mauchly invented Eniac. Following computing machines came punch cards and Grace Hopper's structured analysis and design to support Cobol development. In the 1960s, Smalltalk, an object-oriented language, was invented, and in 1986, Bjarne Stroustrop invented what is now known as C++. It wasn't until around this same time period—the 1980s—that very smart men like Ivar Jacobson, James Rumbaugh, and Grady Booch started defining elements of modern software analysis and design, what we now call the UML.

In the late 1980s and early 1990s, modeling notation wars were in full gear, with different factions supporting Jacobson, Rumbaugh, or Booch. Remember, it wasn't until 1980 that the average person could purchase and own—and do something useful with—a personal computer (PC). Jacobson, Rumbaugh, and Booch each used different symbols and rules to create their models. Finally, Rumbaugh and Booch began collaborating on elements of their respective modeling languages, and Jacobson joined them at Rational Software.

In the mid-1990s, the modeling elements of Rumbaugh [Object Modeling Technique (OMT)], Booch (Booch method), and Jacobson (Objectory and Use Cases)—Rumbaugh, Jocobson, and Rumbaugh are referred to as "the three amigos"—were merged together to form the *unified modeling process*. Shortly thereafter, *process* was removed from the modeling specification, and the UML was born. This occurred very recently, in just 1997. The UML 2.0 specification stabilized in October 2004; that's right, we are just now on version 2.

This begs the question: Just how many companies are using the UML and actually designing software with models? The answer is still very few. I work all over North America and personally know people in some very successful software companies, and when I ask them if they build software with the UML, the answer is almost always no.

If No One Is Modeling, Why Should You?

A rational person might ask: Why then, if Bill Gates is making billions writing software without a significant emphasis on formal modeling, should I care about the UML? The answer is that almost 80 percent of all software projects fail. These projects exceed their budgets, don't provide the features customers need or desire, or worse, are never delivered.

The current trend is to outsource software development to developing or third-world nations. The basic idea is that if American software engineers are failing, then perhaps paying one-fifth for a Eurasian software developer will permit companies to try five times as often to succeed. What are these outsourcing companies finding? They are discovering that the United States has some of the best talent and resources available and that cheap labor in far-away places only introduces additional problems and is no guarantee of success either. The real answer is that more time needs to be spent on software analysis and design, and this means models.

Modeling and the Future of Software Development

A growing emphasis on formal analysis and design does not mean the end of the software industry's growth. It does mean that the wild, wild west days of the 1980s and 1990s eventually will come to a close, but it is still the wild, wild hacking west out there in software land and will be for some time.

What an increasing emphasis on software analysis and design means right now is that trained UML practitioners have a unique opportunity to capitalize on this growing interest in the UML. It also means that gradually fewer projects will fail, software quality should improve, and more software engineers will be expected to learn the UML.

Modeling Tools

Until very recently, modeling has been a captive in an ivory tower surrounded by an impenetrable garrison of scientists armed with metamodels and ridiculously expensive modeling tools. The cost of one license for a popular modeling tool was in the thousands of dollars; this meant that the average practitioner would have to spend as much on one application for modeling as he or she spent for an entire computer. This is ridiculous.

Modeling tools can be very useful, but it is possible to model on scraps of paper. Thankfully, you don't have to go that far. Love it or hate it, Microsoft is very good at driving down the cost of software. If you have a copy of MSDN, then you have a modeling tool that is almost free, Visio. Visio is a good tool, ably capable of producing high-quality UML models, and it won't break your budget.[1]

In keeping with the theme of this book—demystifying UML—instead of breaking the bank on Together or Rose, we are going to use the value-priced Visio. If you want to use Rose XDE, Together, or some other product, you are welcome to do so, but after reading this book, you will see that you can use Visio and create professional models and save yourself hundreds or even thousands of dollars.

Using Models

Models consist of diagrams and pictures. The intent of models is that they are cheaper to produce and experiment with than code. However, if you labor over what models to draw, when to stop drawing and start coding, or whether your models are perfect or not, then you will slowly watch the cost and time value of models dwindle away.

You can use plain text to describe a system, but more information can be conveyed with pictures. You could follow the eXtreme Programming (XP) dictum and code away, refactoring as you go, but the details of lines of code are much more complex than pictures, and programmers get attached to code but not to pictures. (I don't completely understand the psychology of this code attachment, but it really does exist. Just try to constructively criticize someone else's code, and watch the conversation deteriorate very quickly into name calling.) This means that once code is written, it is very hard to get buy-in from its coder or a manager to make modifications, especially if the code is perceived to work. Conversely, people will gladly tinker with models and accept suggestions.

Finally, because models use simple symbols, more stakeholders can participate in design of the system. Show an end user a hundred lines of code, and you can hear the crickets chirping; show such an end user an activity diagram, and that same person can tell you if you have captured the essence of how that task is performed correctly.

---

[1]Microsoft has a new program that permits you to purchase MSDN Universal, which includes Visio, for $375. This is an especially good value.

Creating Diagrams

The first rule of creating models is that code and text are time-consuming, and we don't want to spend a lot of time creating text documents that no one wants to read. What we do want to do is to capture the important parts of the problem and a solution accurately. Unfortunately, this is not a prescription for the number or variety of diagrams we need to create, and it does not indicate how much detail we need to add to those diagrams.

Toward the end of this chapter, in the section "Finding the finsh line.", I will talk more about how one knows that one has completed modelling. Right now, let's talk about the kinds of diagram we may want to create.

Reviewing Kinds of Diagrams

There are several kinds of diagrams that you can create. I will quickly review the kinds of diagrams you can create and the kinds of information each of these diagrams is intended to convey.

Use Case Diagrams

Use case diagrams are the equivalent of modern cave art. A use case's main symbols are the *actor* (our friend Esaw) and the *use case oval* (Figure 1-2).

Use case diagrams are responsible primarily for documenting the macro requirements of the system. Think of use case diagrams as the list of capabilities the system must provide.

Activity Diagrams

An *activity diagram* is the UML version of a flowchart. Activity diagrams are used to analyze processes and, if necessary, perform process reengineering (Figure 1-3).

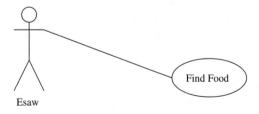

Figure 1-2   The "FindFood" use case.

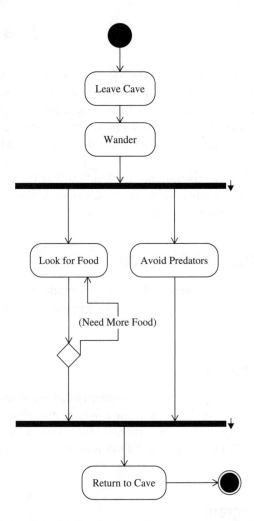

Figure 1-3 An activity diagram showing how Esaw goes about finding food.

An activity diagram is an excellent tool for analyzing problems that the system ultimately will have to solve. As an analysis tool, we don't want to start solving the problem at a technical level by assigning classes, but we can use activity diagrams to understand the problem and even refine the processes that comprise the problem.

Class Diagrams

Class diagrams are used to show the classes in a system and the relationships between those classes (Figure 1-4). A single class can be shown in more than one class

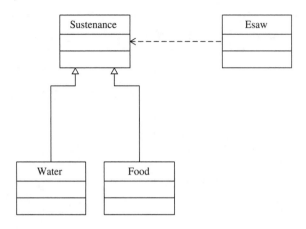

Figure 1-4   A single class diagram, perhaps one of many, that conveys a facet of the system being designed.

diagram, and it isn't necessary to show all the classes in a single, monolithic class diagram. The greatest value is to show classes and their relationships from various perspectives in a way that will help convey the most useful understanding.

Class diagrams show a static view of the system. Class diagrams do not describe behaviors or how instances of the classes interact. To describe behaviors and interactions between objects in a system, we can turn to *interaction diagrams*.

Interaction Diagrams

There are two kinds of interaction diagrams, the *sequence* and the *collaboration.* These diagrams convey the same information, employing a slightly different perspective. Sequence diagrams show the classes along the top and messages sent between those classes, modeling a single flow through the objects in the system. Collaboration diagrams use the same classes and messages but are organized in a spatial display. Figure 1-5 shows a simple example of a sequence diagram, and Figure 1-6 conveys the same information using a collaboration diagram.

A sequence diagram implies a time ordering by following the sequence of messages from top left to bottom right. Because the collaboration diagram does not indicate a time ordering visually, we number the messages to indicate the order in which they occur.

Some tools will convert interaction diagrams between sequence and collaboration automatically, but it isn't necessary to create both kinds of diagrams. Generally, a sequence diagram is perceived to be easier to read and more common.

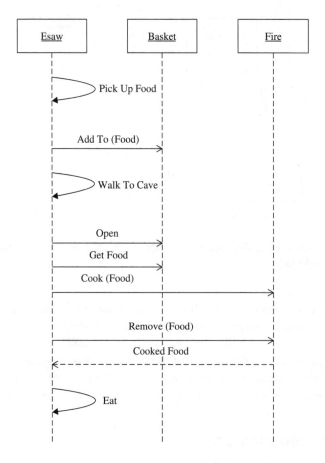

Figure 1-5 A single sequence diagram demonstrating how food is gathered and prepared.

State Diagrams

Whereas interaction diagrams show objects and the messages passed between them, a *state diagram* shows the changing state of a single object as that object passes through a system. If we continue with our example, then we will focus on Esaw and how his state is changing as he forages for food, finds food, and consumes it (Figure 1-7).

REMEMBER *Demystified—the UML is a language. Like programming or spoken languages, idioms that you don't use frequently may become a little rusty from disuse. It is perfectly acceptable to look up a particular idiom. The goal of modeling is to capture the essence of modeling and to design proficiently and, ultimately, as accurately as possible without getting stuck arbitrating language elements. Unfortunately, UML tools aren't as accurate as compilers in describing language errors.*

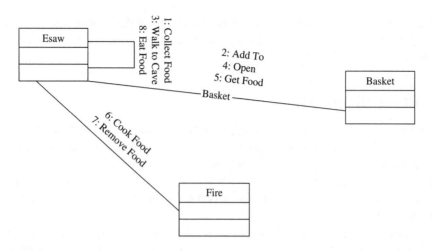

Figure 1-6   A collaboration diagram that conveys the same gathering and consuming behavior.

Component Diagrams

The UML defines various kinds of models, including analysis, design, and implementation models. However, there is nothing forcing you to create or maintain three models for one application. An example of a diagram you might find in an implementation model is a component diagram. A *component diagram* shows the components—think subsystems—in the final product.

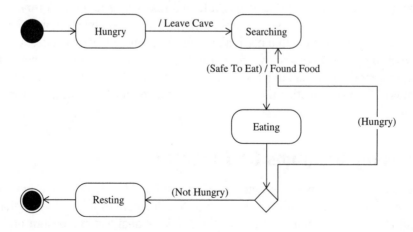

Figure 1-7   A state diagram (or *statechart*) showing the progressive state as Esaw forages and eats.

I'll cover deployment diagrams later in this book but defer citing an example for now. Generally, a component diagram is a bit like a class diagram with component symbols.

Other Diagrams

There are other kinds or variations of diagrams we can create. For example, a *deployment topology diagram* will show you what your system will look like deployed. Such a diagram typically contains symbols representing things such as Web servers, database servers, and various and sundry devices and software that make up your solution. This kind of diagram is more common when you are building *n*-tiered distributed systems.

I will show you examples of some of these diagrams later in this book. Remember that the key to modeling is to modeling interesting aspects of your system that help to clarify elements that may not be obvious, as opposed to modeling everything.

Finding the Finish Line

The hardest part of modeling is that it is so new that UML models are subjected to some of the same language wars object-oriented projects suffered from during the last decade. I encourage you to avoid these language wars as mostly unproductive academic exercises. If you find yourself getting hung up on whether something is or isn't good UML, then you are heading toward analysis (and design) paralysis.

The goal is to be as accurate as possible in a reasonable amount of time. Poorly designed software is bad enough, but no software is almost always worse. To determine if you are finished with a particular diagram or model, ask the question: *Does the diagram or model convey my understanding, meaning, and intent?* That is, is the diagram or model good enough? Accuracy is important because others need to read your models, and idiomatic mistakes mean that the models will be harder for others to read.

How Many Diagrams Do I Create?

There is no specific answer. A better question is: *Do I have to create every kind of diagram?* The answer to this question is no. A refinement of this answer is that it is helpful to create diagrams that resolve persnickety analysis and design problems and diagrams that people actually will read.

How Big Should a Diagram Be?

Determining how big a model needs to be is another good question to decide. If a given model is too big, then it may add to confusion. Try to create detailed models—but not too detailed. As with programming, creating UML models takes practice.

Solicit feedback from different constituencies. If the end users think that an analysis diagram adequately and correctly captures the problem, then move on. If the programmers can read a sequence and figure out how to implement that sequence, then move on. You can always add details if you must.

How Much Text Should Supplement My Models?

A fundamental idea for using pictures for modeling instead of long-winded text is that pictures convey more meaning in a smaller space and are easier to manipulate. If you add too much text—constraints, notes, or long documents—then you are defeating the purpose of this more concise pictorial notation.

The best place for text is the use case. A good textual description in each use case can clarify precisely what feature that use case supports. I will demonstrate some good use case descriptions in Chapter 2.

You are welcome to add any clarifying text you need, but the general rule for text is analogous to the rule for comments in code: Only comment things that are reasonably subject to interpretation.

Finally, try to document everything in your modeling tool as opposed to a separate document. If you find that you need or the customer requires a written architectural overview, defer this until after the software has been produced.

Get a Second Opinion

If you find yourself getting stuck on a particular diagram, get a second opinion. Often, putting a diagram aside for a couple of hours or getting a second opinion will help you to resolve issues about one model. You may find that the end user of that model will understand your meaning or provide more information that clears up the confusion, or a second set of eyes may yield a ready response. A critical element to all software development is to build some inertia and capture the macro, or big, concepts without getting stuck or keeping users waiting.

Contrasting Modeling Languages with Process

The UML actually began life as the Unified Process. The inventors quickly realized that programming languages do not dictate process, and neither should modeling languages. Hence process and language were divided.

There are many books on process. I don't think one process represents the best fit for all projects, but perhaps one of the more flexible processes is the Rational Unified Process. My focus in this book is on the UML, not on any particular process. I will be suggesting the kinds of models to create and what they tell you, but I encourage you to explore development processes for yourself. Consider exploring the Rational Unified Process (RUP), the Agile process, eXtreme Programming (XP), and even Microsoft's Services Oriented Architecture (SOA). (SOA is more of an architectural approach using elements like XML Web Services, but it offers some good techniques.)

I am not an expert on every process, but here is a summary that will provide you with a starting point. The RUP is a buffet of activities centered on the UML that defines iterative, small waterfalls macro phases, including inception, elaboration, construction, and transition. XP is constructive hacking. The idea generally is based on building on your understanding, expecting things to change, and using techniques such as refactoring and pair programming to support changes as your understanding grows. Microsoft's SOA depends on technologies like COM+, Remoting, and XML Web Services and a separation of responsibilities by services. Agile is a new methodology that I don't understand completely, but Dr. Boehm's book, *Balancing Agility and Discipline*, compares it with XP, and I suspect that conceptually it lives somewhere between RUP and XP.

It is important to keep in mind that many of the people or entities offering a process may be trying to sell you something, and some very good ideas have come from each of these parties.

Quiz

1. What does the acronym UML mean?

    a. Uniform Model Language

    b. Unified Modeling Language

    c. Unitarian Mock-Up Language

    d. Unified Molding Language

2. The UML is used only to model software.

   a. True

   b. False

3. What is the name of the process most closely associated with the UML?

   a. The modeling process

   b. The Rational Unified Process

   c. eXxtreme Programming

   d. Agile methods

4. What is the name of the standards body that defines the UML?

   a. Unified Modeling Group

   b. Object Modeling Group

   c. Object Management Group

   d. The Four Amigos

5. Use case diagrams are used to capture macro descriptions of a system.

   a. True

   b. False

6. Sequence diagrams differ from collaboration diagrams (choose all that apply).

   a. Sequence diagrams are interaction diagrams; collaboration diagrams are not.

   b. Sequence diagrams represent a time ordering, and collaboration diagrams represent classes and messages, but time ordering is not implied.

   c. Time order is indicating by numbering sequence diagrams.

   d. None of the above

7. A class diagram is a dynamic view of the classes in a system.

   a. True

   b. False

8. A good UML model will contain at lest one of every kind of diagram.

   a. True

   b. False

9. What is the nickname of the group of scientists most notably associated with the UML?

   a. The Gang of Four

   b. The Three Musketeers

   c. The Three Amigos

   d. The Dynamic Duo

10. Sequence diagrams are good at showing the state of an object across many use cases.

   a. True

   b. False

Answers

1. b
2. b
3. b
4. c
5. a
6. b
7. b
8. b
9. c
10. b

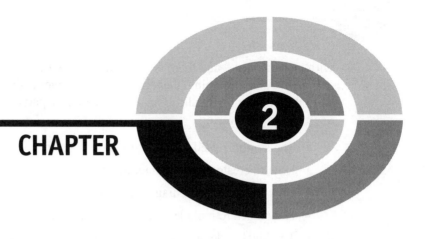

Start at the Beginning with Use Cases

The Unified Modeling Language (UML) supports object-oriented analysis and design by providing you with a way to capture the results of analysis and design. In general, we start with understanding our problem, i.e., analysis. An excellent type of model for capturing analysis is the use case diagram.

The purpose of a *use case* is to describe how a system will be used—to describe its essential purposes. The purpose of use case *diagrams* is to capture the essential purposes visually.

A well-written and well-diagrammed use case is one of the single most important kinds of models you can create. This is so because clearly stating, knowing, and organizing the objectives is singularly important to attaining those objectives successfully. There is an old proverb that says, "A journey of a thousand miles begins with a single step," and there is a slightly younger proverb that says, "If you don't know where you're going, then the journey is never ending."

In this chapter I will talk about a significant first part of such a journey—creating use cases—by covering

- The symbols used to create use case diagrams
- How to create use case diagrams
- How many use case diagrams to create
- How much to include in a use case diagram
- The level of detail to include in a use case diagram
- How to express relationships between individual use cases
- The quantity and style of text that is useful for annotating use case diagrams
- Significantly, how to prioritize use cases

Making the Case for Use Cases

Use case diagrams look deceptively simple. They consist of stick figures, lines, and ovals. The stick figure is called an *actor* and represents someone or something that acts on the system. In software development, actors are people or other software that acts on the system. The lines are dotted or solid lines, with or without various arrows that indicate the relationship between the actor and the ovals. The ovals are the use cases, and in the use case diagram, these ovals have some text that provides a basic description. Figure 2-1 is a simple example of a use case diagram.

For a long time use case diagrams bugged me. They did so because they seemed too simple to be of any value. A child of three or four with a crayon and a piece of paper could reproduce these stick figures. Their simplicity is the deception, however.

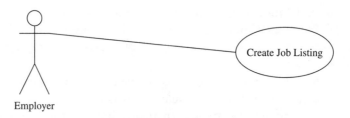

Figure 2-1   A very simple use case diagram.

That a use case diagram is easy to create is implicit praise for the UML. Finding the right use cases and recording their responsibilities correctly is the deception. Finding the right use cases and describing them adequately is the critical process that prevents clever software engineers from skipping critical requirements and inventing unnecessarily. In a nutshell, use case diagrams are a macro record of what you want to build.

In the preceding paragraph, I used the word *macro*. Macro in this context simply means "big." The big, or macro, objectives are what are referred to as compelling business arguments, or reasons, for doing something. Use case diagrams capture the big, compelling objectives. The use case text captures supporting details.

This is what I missed in the stick figure pictures of use case diagrams. I missed that simply by recording what the system will do and what it won't do, we record and specify the scope of what we are creating. I also missed that the text that accompanies use case diagrams fills in the blanks between the macro uses and the micro uses, where *micro* means "smaller, supporting" uses.

In addition to recording the primary and secondary uses, use case diagrams implicitly provide us with several significant opportunities for managing development, which I will go into in more detail as the chapter progresses.

Prioritizing Capabilities

Have you ever written a to-do list? A *to-do list* is a list of things that you must do or desire to do. The act of writing the list is a starting point. Use cases are essentially to-do lists. Once you have captured the use cases, you have articulated what the system will do, and you can use the list to prioritize our tasks. Both stating and organizing objectives are very critical early tasks.

The value in prioritizing the capabilities of a system is that software is fluid. Let me illustrate what I mean by example. It is possible to create, save, open, and print a text document with both Notepad and Microsoft Word, but the difference in the number of lines of code and the number of features between these two programs is tremendous. By prioritizing uses, we often have the opportunity to juggle features, budget, and schedule advantageously.

Suppose, for example, that my primary objectives are to be able to create, save, open, and print a text document. Further suppose that my secondary objectives are to save the document as plain text, HyperText Markup Language (HTML), and rich text—i.e., special formatting. Prioritizing the capabilities means that I could elect to focus on primary uses—create, save, open, and print—but defer supporting HTML and rich text. (Features in software commonly are deferred to later versions owing to the real constraints mentioned earlier, including, time, budget, and a change in the business environment.)

Not having enough time and running out of money are straightforward problems. Software developers are routinely optimistic, get distracted by tangents, and spend more time in meetings than planned, and these things tax a budget. However, let's take a moment to examine a change in the business environment. If our original requirements were HTML, plain text, and rich text and we were building our software in the last 5 years, it is perfectly plausible that a customer might say, during the middle of development, that saving a document as eXtensible Markup Language (XML) text would be more valuable than rich text. Thus, owing to an evolving technological climate, midstream a customer might reprioritize and demand XML as more important than rich text. Had we not documented our primary and secondary requirements, then it might be very challenging to determine desirable tradeoffs, such as swapping rich text for XML. Because we clearly recorded desirable use cases, we are able to prioritize and make valuable tradeoffs if we have to.

Communicating with Nontechnophiles

Another thing that I missed about use cases is that their very simplicity makes them an easy conveyance for communicating with nontechnophiles. We call these people *users* or *customers*.

Left-brained programmers generally loathe users. The basic idea is that if one cannot read code, then one is dumb or, at least, dumber than those who can. The UML and use cases bridge the gap between left-brained programmers and nontechnophile users.

A stick figure, line, and oval are simplistic enough, when combined with some text, that every participant can understand the meaning. The result is that users and customers can look at the drawings and read the plain text and determine if the technologists have accurately recorded and understand the desirable features or not. This also means that managers—who may have not written code in 10 years—and technical leads can examine the end product and by inspection ensure that rampant inventiveness isn't the cause of missed schedules or absent features. Demonstrating this dissonance by continuing my earlier example, suppose that rich text support is implemented anyway because the programmer knows how to store and retrieve rich text. However, because XML is newer and the programmer has less experience working with XML, the XML write feature is unmaliciously deferred. A proactive manager can track a customer's needs as captured by the use cases and preempt unproductive tangents.

Because use cases are visual and simple, users and customers can provide feedback, and bridge-persons between customers and programmers, such as managers, can determine if features actually built accurately reflect the desires of users.

Using Use Case Symbols

Basic use case diagrams consist of just a few symbols. These are the *actor*, a *connector*, and the *use case oval* (Figure 2-2). Let's take a few minutes to talk about how these symbols are used and what information they convey.

Actor Symbols

The stick figure, referred to as an *actor*, represents participants in use cases. Actors can be people or things. If an actor is a person, then it may never actually be represented by code. If an actor is another subsystem, then the actor may be realized as a class or subprogram but still be represented using the actor symbol in use case diagrams.

Actors are discovered as a result of analysis. As you are identifying the macro uses of the system, you will identify who the participants for those use cases are. Initially, record each actor as it is discovered by adding an actor symbol to your model and describing what the actor's role is. We will worry about organization and refinement later in the section entitled, "Creating Use Case Diagrams."

Use Cases

The use case symbol is used to represent capabilities. The use case is given a name and a text description. The text should describe how the use case starts and ends and include a description of the capability described by the use case name, as well as supporting scenarios and nonfunctional requirements. We will explore examples of use case names in the section entitled, "Creating Use Case Diagrams," and I will provide a template outline that you can use to help you write use case descriptions in the section entitled, "Documenting a Use Case Using an Outline."

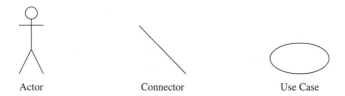

Actor   Connector   Use Case

Figure 2-2   Basic use case diagram symbols include the actor, the connector, and the use case oval.

Connectors

Because use case diagrams can have multiple actors, and because use cases can be associated with actors and other use cases, use case connectors are used to indicate how actors and use cases are associated. In addition, connector styles can change to convey more information about the relationship between actors and use cases. Finally, connectors can have additional adornments and annotations that provide even more information.

Connector Line Styles

There are three basic connector line styles. A plain-line connector is called an *association* and is used to show which actors are related to which use cases. For example, Figure 2-1 showed that an employer is associated with the use case "Create a Job Listing."

A second connector style is a dashed line with a directional arrow (Figure 2-3). This style of connector is referred to as a *dependency*. The arrow points to the use case that is depended on. For example, suppose that employers in *www.motown-jobs.com* have to be logged in to create a job listing. Then we can say that the use case "Create a Job Listing" depends on a use case "Log-In." This is the relationship depicted in Figure 2-3.

A third connector style is a directed line with a hollow triangle. This is called a *generalization*. The word *generalization* in the UML means "inheritance." When we show a generalization relationship between two actors or two use cases, then we are indicating that the child actor or use case is an instance of the base actor or use and something more. Figure 2-4 shows a generalization relationship between two actors and two use cases.

In generalization relationships, the arrow points toward the thing on which we are expanding. There are a number of ways you can describe this relationship

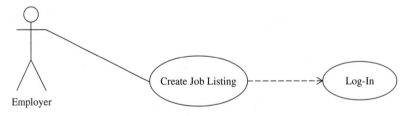

Figure 2-3   The use case "Create a Job Listing" depends on the employer logging in.

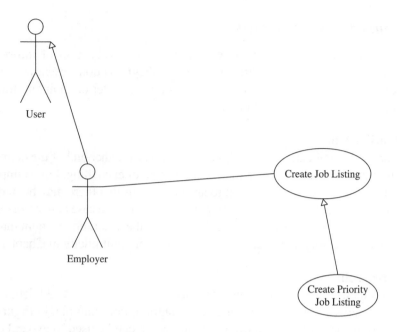

Figure 2-4   A use case diagram showing two generalization relationships between two actors and two use cases.

verbally—which you should know about—but unfortunately, all these synonyms can lead to verbal confusion. The following statements describe the generalization relationships shown in Figure 2-4:

- User is the target, and Employer is the source.
- Employer *is* a User.
- User is the subtype, and Employer is the supertype.
- Employer inherits from User.
- User is the parent type, and Employer is the child type.
- Employer generalizes User.

(In this list you can substitute the phrase *Create a Job Listing* everywhere you see the word *User* and substitute the phrase *Create Priority Job Listing* everywhere you see the word *Employer* to convey the relationship between the two use cases.) The latter statement, which uses the word *generalizes*, is the most accurate in the context of the UML, but it is worth recognizing that all the statements are equivalent.

Connector Adornments

UML diagrams encourage less text because pictures convey a lot of information through a convenient visual shorthand, but UML diagrams don't eschew text altogether. For example, connectors can include text that indicates endpoint multiplicity and text that stereotypes the connector.

Showing Multiplicity

Connectors in general can have multiplicity notations at either end of the connector. The multiplicity notations indicate the possible count of each thing. For example, an asterisk means many. An asterisk next to an actor means that there may be many instances of that actor. Although the UML permits notating use case connectors in this way, it isn't that common. You are more likely to see these notational count marks in such diagrams as class diagrams, so I will elaborate on multiplicity in Chapter 3.

Stereotyping Connectors

A more common connector notation is the stereotype. Stereotypes add detail to the relationship between elements in a use case diagram. For example, in Figure 2-3, I introduced the dependency connector. A stereotype can be used to expand on the meaning of the dependency connector.

In the section entitled, "Connector Line Styles," I said that an employer can create a job listing and illustrated this with an employer actor, a "Create Job Listing" use case, and an association connector. However, I also said that the employer must be logged in. When a use case—"Create a Job Listing"—needs the services of another use case—"Log-In"—then the dependent use case is said to *include* the depended-on use case. (In code, an include relationship is implemented as code reuse.)

A stereotype is shown as text between the guillemots (« and » characters). For instance, if we say that "Create a Job Listing" includes "Log-In," then we can depict an include stereotype by annotating the dependency connector as shown in Figure 2-5.

Figure 2-5   An example of an include stereotype—used to depict reuse—on the dependency between "Create Job Listing" and "Log-In."

Include and extend are important concepts in use case diagrams, so I will expand on these subjects next.

NOTE *Stereotype is a generally useful concept in the UML. The reason for this is that it is permissible to introduce and define your own stereotypes. In this way you can extend the UML.*

Including and Extending Use Cases

A dependency relationship between two use cases means that in some way the dependent use case needs the depended-on use case. Two commonly used, predefined stereotypes that refine dependencies in use cases are the include and extend stereotypes. Let's take a minute to expand on our introductory comments on include from the preceding section and introduce extend.

TIP *Visio applies an extends stereotype on the generalization connector to mean inheritance. Variations between the UML and UML tools exist because the UML is an evolving standard, and the implementation of tools may lag or lead the official definition of the UML.*

More on Include Stereotypes

A dependency labeled with the include stereotype means that the dependent use case ultimately is intended to reuse the depended-on use case. The baggage that goes with the include stereotype is that the dependent use case will need the services of and know something about the realization of the depended-on use, but the opposite is not true. The depended-on use case is a whole and distinct entity that must not depend on the dependent use case. Logging in is a good example. It is clear that we require an employer to log in to create a job listing, but we could log in for other reasons too.

NOTE *In an include dependency between use cases, the dependent use case is also referred to as the* base *use case, and the depended-on use case is also referred to as the* inclusion *use case. While* base *and* inclusion *may be more precise, they do not seem to be employed in speech commonly yet.*

Putting so much meaning into a little word like *include* is why the UML can convey a lot of meaning in a simple diagram, but it is also why UML models can be challenging to create and to read. A real strategy that you can fall back on is to add a note where you are not sure about the use of some idiomatic aspect of the UML (see "Attaching Notes to Use Case Diagrams" below.) For example, if you want to describe the relationship between "Create a Job Listing" and "Log-In" but aren't sure about which connector or stereotype to use, then you could use a plain association and a note connected to the connector describing in plain text what you mean. The note can act as a reminder to go back and look up the precise UML later.

Using Extend Stereotypes

The extend stereotype is used to add more detail to a dependency, which means that we are adding more capabilities (see Figure 2-6 for an example). As shown in the figure, we say that "Log Viewed Listings" extends (and is dependent on) "View Listing."

NOTE *In an extend relationship, the arrow points toward the base use case, and the other end is referred to as the* extension use case.

In the preceding section we would not permit an employer to create a job listing without logging in, but the use case log in is indifferent to the use case reusing it. In this section the use case view listing doesn't care that it is being logged; in other words, the logging feature will need to know about the view listing feature, but not vice versa.

A valuable perspective here is who might be interested in the logging. Clearly, the "Job Seeker" probably doesn't care how many times the listing has been viewed, but a prospective employer might be interested in how much traffic his or her listing is generating. Now switch to a different domain for a moment. Suppose that the "Job Seeker" were a home buyer and that a listing were a residential listing. Now both the buyer and seller might be interested in the number of times the property has been viewed. A house that has been on the market for months may have problems. Yet, in both scenarios, the listing is the most important thing, and the number

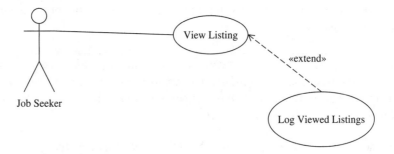

Figure 2-6 Tracking the number of times a job listing is viewed is an extension of "View Listing," as depicted by the dependency and the extend stereotype.

of viewings is secondary. This illustrates the notion of extension use cases as akin to features, and from a marketing perspective, extensions might be items that are separated into an optional feature pack.

TIP   *Consider another alternative as relates to an extension use case. Extension use cases are natural secondary features. If your project has a tight schedule, do the extension use cases last, and if you run out of time, then postpone the extension use cases to a later version.*

Include and extend seem somewhat similar, but the best way to keep them straight is to remember that "the include relationship is intended for reusing behavior modeled by another use case, whereas the extend relationship is intended for adding parts to existing use cases as well as for modeling optional system services" (Övergaard and Palmkvist, 2005, p. 79).

Annotating Use Case Diagrams

Consider the job of a court stenographer. Stenographers use those funny stenographic typewriters that produce a sort of shorthand gibberish. We can safely assume that if a regular typewriter or word processor were capable of accepting input fast enough to keep up with natural speech, then the stenograph would not have been invented.

Stenographs produce shorthand that is more condensed than speech. The UML is like shorthand for code and text, and UML modeling tools are like stenographs. The idea is that models can be created faster than code or faster than writing textual descriptions. That said, sometimes there is no good substitute for text.

If you find yourself in the predicament that only text seems to resolve—or you aren't sure of the UML—then go ahead and add text. You can add text by documenting your models with features of most modeling tools, by adding URL references to more verbose documents, or by adding notes directly in the diagrams themselves. However, if you add too much text, then naturally it will take longer for the modeling to be complete and may require a greater effort to understand the meaning of individual diagrams.

Inserting Notes

The UML is a shorthand for a lot of text and code, but if you need to, you can always add text. Every diagram, including use cases, supports adding textual annotations. Notes are represented as a dog-eared piece of paper with a line attaching the textbox to the element being annotated (Figure 2-7). Use notes sparingly because they can clutter up a diagram and make it harder to read.

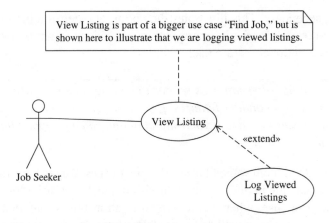

Figure 2-7   A note adding plain text to clarify some aspect of a diagram.

Adding Supporting Documentation

Every modeling tool that I have used—Together, Rose, Rose XDE, Visio, Poseidon for UML, and the one from Cayenne Software—supports model documentation. This documentation usually takes two forms: text that is stored in the model and Uniform Resource Locators (URLs) referencing external documents (Figure 2-8). Exploring the features of your particular tool will uncover these capabilities.

More important is what kind of documentation you should provide. Subjectively, the answer is as little as you can get away with, but use case diagrams generally seem to need the most.

Use case diagrams are pretty basic with their stick figures but are pretty important because they record the capabilities your system will have. Good information to include with your use case diagrams is

- A pithy paragraph describing how the use begins, including any preconditions
- A short paragraph for each of the primary functions
- A short paragraph for each of the secondary functions
- A short paragraph for each of the primary and secondary scenarios, which helps to place the need for the functions in a context
- A paragraph for nonfunctional requirements
- Insertion points where any other dependent use cases are used
- An ending point with postconditions

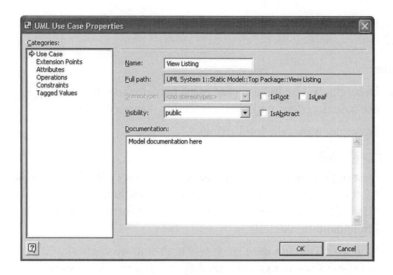

Figure 2-8   By double clicking on a model element in Visio, you can add documentation that is stored in the model.

All these elements sound like a lot of work and can be. Remember, though, that use cases are the foundations of analysis, and it is important to document them as carefully and as thoroughly as you can. It is equally important to note that I used the words *pithy* and *short* intentionally. By short, I mean that it is acceptable to have one-sentence paragraphs.

You can use any format you like for documenting your use cases. If you are comfortable with the outline format, it is very easy to create a template outline from the bulleted list. A good practice is to choose a style for your documentation and stick with it.

Let's take a moment to elaborate on the elements—as described in the preceding bulleted list—of use case documentation. Keep in mind that this is not an exact science, and your use case documentation doesn't have to be perfect.

Documenting a Use Case Using an Outline

You can use free-form text to document a use case, but I find that an outline template suggests the extent of the information and acts as a reminder of the elements needed to document each use case adequately. Here is a template; the template includes a brief description and example for each section. It is worth

noting that this style of documentation is not part of the UML but is a useful part of modeling.

1. Title
   a. Description: Use the use case name here, making it very easy to match use case diagrams with their respective documentation.
   b. Example: Maintain Job Listing

2. Use case starts
   a. Description: Briefly describe the circumstances leading up to the use case, including preconditions. Leave out implementation details, such as "User Clicks a Hyperlink" or references to forms, controls, or specific implementation details.
   b. Example: This use case starts when an employer, employer's agent, or the system wants to create, modify, or remove a job listing.

3. Primary functions
   a. Description: Use cases are not necessarily singular. For example, "Manage Job Listing" is a reasonable use case and may include primary functions such as reading and writing to a repository. The key here is to avoid having too few or too many primary functions. If you need a good yardstick, it might be two or three primary functions per use case.
   b. Example: "CRUD Job Listing." The primary functions of "Maintain Job Listing" are to create, read, update, and delete the job listing.

4. Secondary functions
   a. Description: Secondary functions are like a supporting cast in a play. For example, given a use case "Manage Job Listing," updating, inserting, creating, and deleting a job listing—called *CRUD*, for create, read, update, and delete—are excellent secondary functions, part of a bigger use case. If you need a yardstick, then two times as many secondary functions as primary functions is good.
   b. Examples:
      (1) "Expire Job Listing." Thirty days after the listing is made available for viewing, the listing is said to expire. An expired listing is not deleted, but users, with the exception of the listing owner, may no longer view the listing.
      (2) "Renew Job Listing." A listing may be extended for an additional 30 days by paying an additional listing extension fee.

    (3) "Make Job Listing a Priority Listing." Any time during the life of a listing, the owner of that listing may elect to promote the listing to a priority listing for a fee prorated by the exhausted portion of the listing period.

    (4) "Log Viewed Listing." Each time a listing is viewed, a log entry will be written, recording the date and time the listing was viewed and the Internet Protocol (IP) address of the viewer.

    (5) "Examine View Logs." At any time the owner of a listing may view the logged information for his or her listings.

    (6) "Automatic Viewed-Log Notification." The owner of a job listing may elect to have view logs sent by e-mail at an interval specified by the owner.

    (7) "Pay for Listing." The owner of the listing is required to pay for every listing unless the listing is offered as a promotional giveaway.

5. Primary scenarios

    a. Description and example: A scenario is a short story that describes the functions in a context. For instance, given a primary function "Create Job Listing," we might write a scenario such as this: "Mr. Jones' secretary is retiring, and he needs to hire a replacement. Mr. Jones would like a secretary who types 100 words per minute, is willing to work only four hours per day, and is willing to work for $10 per hour. He needs the replacement secretary to start no later than January 15." Consider at least as many primary scenarios as you have primary functions. Also consider a couple of scenario variations for important functions. This will help you to think about your problem in creative ways. It is a useful practice to list the scenarios in approximately the same order as the functions that the scenario describes.

6. Secondary scenarios

    a. Description and example: Secondary scenarios are short stories that put secondary functions in a context. Consider a secondary scenario we will refer to as "Expire Job Listing." Demonstrated as a scenario, we might write: "Mr. Jones paid for the listing to run for 30 days. After 30 days, the job listing is delisted, and Mr. Jones is notified by e-mail, providing him with an opportunity to renew the listing." We can organize the secondary functions in an ordering consistent with the secondary functions they support.

7. Nonfunctional requirements

   a. Description: Nonfunctional requirements address implicit behaviors, such as how fast something happens or how much data can be transmitted.

   b. Example: An employer's payment is to be processed while he or she waits in a period of time no longer than 60 seconds.

8. Use case ends

   a. Description: This part describes what it means for the use case to be finished.

   b. Example: The use case is over when changes made to the job listing are persisted and the payment has been collected.

How much information you include in the written part of your use cases is really up to you. The UML is silent on this matter, but a process such as the RUP may offer you some guidance on content, quantity, and style of text documentation.

As a final note, it is useful to record ideas about functions and scenarios even if you ultimately elect to discard them. For example, we could add a secondary function that states that "The system shall support a semiautomatic renewal of an expiring job listing" supported by the scenario "Mr. Jones' listing for a new secretary is about to expire. Mr. Jones is notified by e-mail of the impending expiration. By clicking on a link in the e-mail, Mr. Jones' listing is automatically renewed using the same billing and payment information used with the original listing."

By recording and keeping considered ideas, it is possible to make a record of ideas that were considered but may or may not ever be realized. Keeping a record of possibilities prevents you from rehashing ideas as team members come and go.

Finally, it is useful to insert references to depended-on use cases. Rather than repeating an inclusion use case, for example, simply make a reference to the inclusion use case at the point at which it is needed. For example, suppose that paying for a job listing requires an employer to log in. Instead of repeating the "Log-In" use case, we simply make a reference to the "Log-In" use case where it is needed; in this instance we can make a reference to "Log-In" when we talk about paying for the job listing.

Creating Use Case Diagrams

As I mentioned earlier, use cases are design to-do lists. Since another holiday is always just around the corner, a good comparative analogy is that defining use cases is like writing a list of chores in order to prepare your house for an extended visit from relatives. For example, you might write down, "Dust living room." Then you decide that your 10-year-old daughter did a good job the last time, so you assign the dusting to her. The level of detail is important here because you know—if you have ever dusted—that different kinds of things need different kinds of dusting. Small knickknacks can be dusted with a feather duster. Coffee tables and end tables might need Pledge® and a clean, dry, cloth, and ceiling fans might need the wand and brush on a vacuum cleaner. The key here is the difference between what we diagram and what we write as part of our use case.

NOTE *You might wonder what dusting has to do with use cases and software. The first answer is that use case models can be used for things that aren't software, and the second part is that software is found in an increasingly larger number of devices. Suppose that we were defining use cases for a house-cleaning robot; then our dusting rules might be useful. And if you are wondering how probable software for robots might be, then consider the Roomba® cleaner. Roomba is a small robot that wanders around a room vacuuming up debris, and according to its marketing material, it even knows when to recharge itself. Someone had to define and implement those capabilities.*

The use case for dusting in the preceding paragraph would consist of an actor, "Child," an association connector, and a use case "Dust Living Room" (Figure 2-9). The use case diagram itself need not depict all the necessary micro tasks that "Dust Living Room" consists of. For example, "Find Pledge and clean, dry cloth" is a necessary subtask but not really a use case in and of itself. Good use cases mean finding good actors and the right level of detail without convoluting the diagrams.

After we have the use case diagram, we can add supporting information in the model documentation for our use case. Primary functions would include dusting key areas, and secondary functions would include preparation, such as getting the vacuum cleaner out and finding the Pledge. Adequate scenarios would include addressing specific problem areas, such as dusting picture frames and collectible items. Nonfunctional requirements might include "Finish dusting before grandparents arrive."

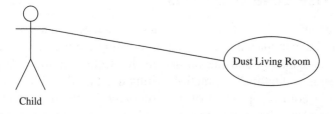

Figure 2-9 The use case for a child actor and dusting a living room.

Don't worry about perfect use case diagrams and use case documentation. Use the outline to help you consider the details and use case diagrams to provide you with a good picture of your objectives.

How Many Diagrams Is Enough?

Sufficiency is a tricky problem. If you provide too many use cases, your modeling can go on for months or even years. You can run into the same problem with use case documentation, too.

NOTE *I consulted on a project for a large department of defense agency. The agency literally had been working on use cases for almost 2 years with no end in sight. Aside from what seemed like a never-ending project, the domain experts felt that the wrong use cases were being captured or that the use cases had little or no explanatory, practical value. The models were missing the mark. The objective is to capture the essential characteristics of your objective, and use case models are an excellent low-tech way to get nontechnical domain experts involved. Skipping the dialogue-provoking value of use case diagrams is missing half the value of the use case diagrams.*

A reasonable baseline is that medium-complexity applications might have between 20 and 50 good use cases. If you know that your problem is moderately complex and you have five use cases, then you may be missing critical functionality. On the other hand, if you have hundreds of use cases, then you may be subdividing practical macro use cases into micro use cases.

Unfortunately, there are no hard and fast rules. Defining the right use cases takes practice and requires good judgment that is acquired over time. To help you begin acquiring some experience, the next subsection demonstrates some actual use case diagrams for *www.motown-jobs.com*.

Example Use Case Diagrams

This book is about the UML. Specific text documentation is not part of the UML, so I will limit the examples in this section to creating the use case diagrams. You can use your imagination and the outline in the section entitled "Documenting a Use Case Using an Outline" to practice writing use case descriptions.

Motown-jobs.com is a product of my company, Software Conceptions, Inc. Motown-jobs is a Web site for matching people looking for jobs with people offering jobs. It is a Web site like dice.com, monster.com, computerjobs.com, or hotjobs.com and is implemented in ASP.NET. All this aside, Motown-jobs.com started as an idea whose features were captured as a group of use cases. Because I was building the software for my company, I had to play the role of domain expert—the domain being what it takes to match employers with employees. Since I have been looking for and finding customers for my company for 15 years, I have some experience in this area.

Finding use cases can start with an interview with your domain expert or by making a list. Since I was playing the role of interviewer and interviewee, I simply began with a list of the things I thought Motown-jobs.com would need to offer to be useful. Here is my list:

- Employers or employers' agents will want to post information about jobs being offered.

- Those looking for jobs may want to post a résumé that can be viewed by potential employers.

- Employers or employers' agents will want to actively search the Web site for résumés that match the skills needed to fill job openings.

- Those looking for jobs will want to search through jobs listed.

- Employers and employers' agents will have to pay for listings and for searching for résumés, but posting résumés or searching through jobs will be a free service.

- An additional source of revenue might be advertising and résumé-building services, so the Web site will be able to sell and post advertising space and help job seekers create résumés.

In addition to software being expensive to write and hardware, server software, and high-speed Internet connections being expensive to purchase and maintain, helping businesses find employees is a valuable service—or at least that is the premise behind building Motown-jobs.com in the first place. Figuring out how much to charge for the listings and attracting advertisers are business and marketing functions, so I won't talk about that in my list of use cases.

Now, clearly, I could get stuck examining all the little tasks that each of the macro tasks—such as posting job vacancies—consists of, but the list I have is a very good starting place. Let's start by diagramming these features (Figure 2-10).

Notice in the Figure 2-10 that I captured maintaining jobs and finding résumés for employer types, maintaining advertisements for advertiser types, posting résumés and finding jobs for job seeker types, and managing billing for the system. The next thing I can do is ask involved parties if these use cases capture the essence of the features I need.

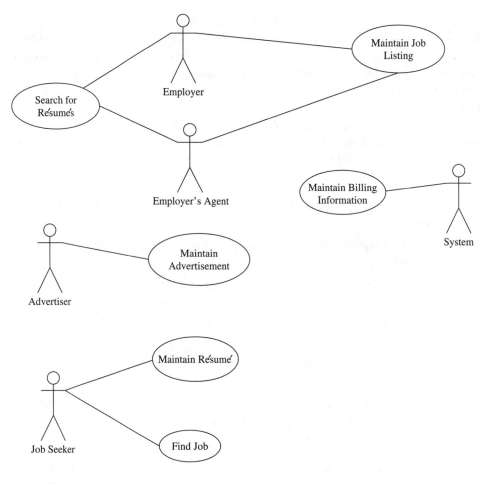

Figure 2-10   A first pass at the use case diagram for Motown-jobs.com.

As a use case diagram, I give this a grade of a C, but it is a start. The next thing I can do is look at the actors and use cases themselves and look for redundancies, simplifications, or needed additional details and make necessary adjustments to the use case diagram.

Defining Actors

In the use case diagram in Figure 2-10, I have "Employer" and "Employer's Agent" actors. However, for all intents and purposes, these two actors do the same things relative to the system, and they do them the same way. Thus I can eliminate "Employer's Agent" and rename "Employer" to "Job Owner"; with a simple description,

"Job Owner" captures the idea that a listed job is "owned" by a responsible party. Figure 2-11 shows the revision in the use case diagram.

Next, it seems pretty obvious that a job listing, a résumé, and an advertisement are all kinds of listings, and the people who own those elements are "Listing Owners." I can experiment with these relationships using generalization. The modified use case diagram is shown in Figure 2-12.

Figure 2-12 treats jobs, advertisements, and résumés all as listings that need to be maintained. It also shows that the billing system is associated with listings and résumé searches. In some ways Figure 2-12 is an improvement, but in others it is too clever. For example, depicting a job seeker as a "Listing Owner" suggests that every job seeker owns a listed résumé. What if a job seeker doesn't want to post

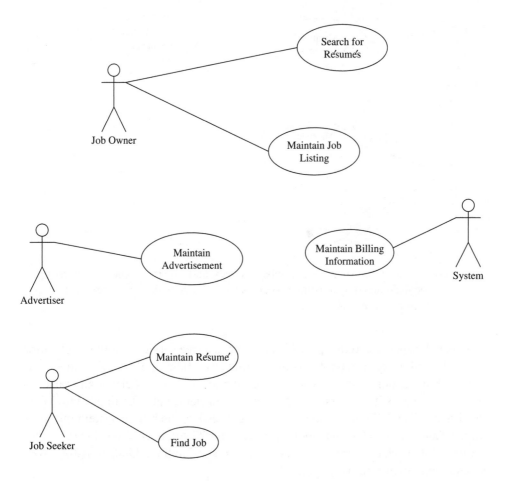

Figure 2-11   "Employer" and "Employer's Agent" are converted to a single actor, "Job Owner."

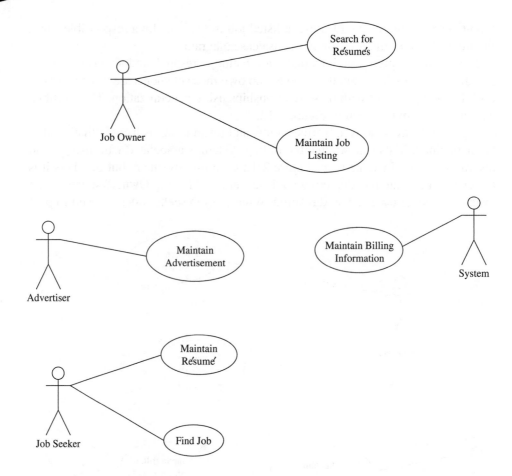

Figure 2-12 This figure suggests that jobs, résumés, and advertisements are all listings that have to be maintained by a listing owner, as well as associations between the billing system and listings and résumé searches.

a résumé? Further, I said that posting a résumé is a free service, but the implication is that the billing system treats résumé listings as a billable item. Does this mean that it is billable but costs $0? The revised diagram seems a bit clever and raises as many questions as it answers. Perhaps I could further divide "Listings" into "Billable Listings" and "Free Listings." This might resolve the billing system question, but what about job seekers who don't post résumés? I still have to resolve this issue. For now, I go back to four separate actors as opposed to three kinds of listing owners and the system actor (Figure 2-13).

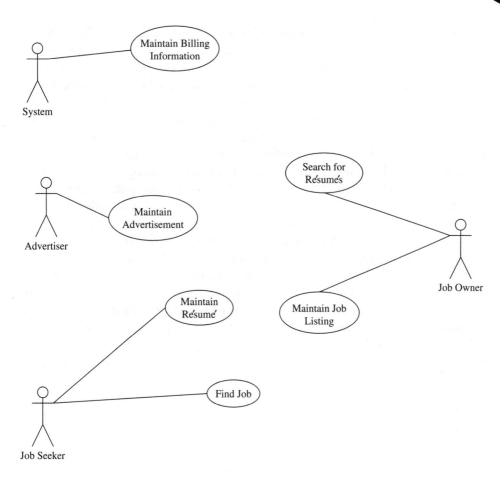

Figure 2-13   Four separate unrelated actors participating in unrelated use cases.

I like the simpler form of the use case diagram in Figure 2-13. It is less cluttered, easier to follow, and tells me what I need to know about the system features.

Dividing Use Cases into Multiple Diagrams

You can elect to have one master use case diagram and several smaller use case diagrams or just several smaller use case diagrams. It is up to you. Simpler diagrams are easier to manage and follow but may not show how use cases are related. I generally prefer separate, simple diagrams and create a single master diagram if I am sure that I will derive some specific benefit from doing so.

In my Motown-jobs.com example I have four significant facets. I have the job seeker–related use cases, job owner–related use cases, use cases for advertisers, and the billing system. To explore each of these facets of the system, I will separate these use cases and their incumbent actors into separate diagrams and add details. Figures 2-14 through 2-17 show the new diagrams.

By separating "Maintain Billing Information" into a separate use case, I have room to add details. For example, it makes sense that the billing system is only interested in billable things and that an actor called a "Registered User" can maintain billable items. Notice that I added the "Log-In" use case. Because I need to know who users are in order to bill them, I will need a means of registering and authenticating.

In Figure 2-15, I introduce the idea that a job seeker is also considered a registered user. However, I elect to require registration only if the user wants to post a résumé. I want to know who people putting information on our system are, but I don't require it of casual browsers. Again, to post something on the system, I will require the user to log in and otherwise only offer the casual user the opportunity to register. The concept of a registered user suggests that I need another use case "Maintain Registration Information." This can be implemented as a simple use case diagram with the "Registered User" actor and an association to the new use case.

In Figure 2-16, I show that an advertiser is a registered user, and I also include that "Maintain Advertisement" generalizes "Maintain Billable Item." Because

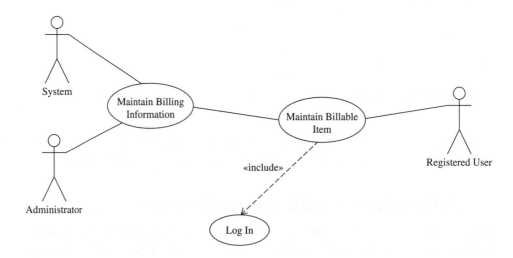

Figure 2-14 This figure shows that a new actor called a "Registered User" can maintain a billable item if he or she is logged in and the billing system is associated with billable items.

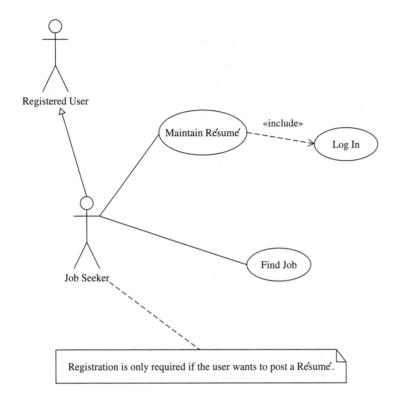

Figure 2-15 An expanded view of use cases related to job seekers.

"Maintain Billable Item" is in the diagram in Figure 2-16, I also know that this means that I am tied to the billing, registration, and authentication (or logging in) use cases, but I intentionally removed those elements from the diagram to unclutter it.

In Figure 2-17, I show the dependency between "Maintain Billable Item" and "Log-In" by showing the dependency connector between these two use cases. It should be obvious that since "Search for Résumés" and "Maintain Job Listing" generalize "Maintain Billable Item," authentication is required to post jobs and search for résumés. Using the single connector simplifies the diagram.

You certainly are welcome to try to create a single master use case diagram, but you don't have to do so. Even in this relatively simple system, a single monolithic model might only add to confusion; our objective is to reduce confusion and increase understanding as simply and as directly as possible. I think that these four models do this, but the discussion illustrates precisely the kinds of issues you will have to weigh when deciding which models to spend time on.

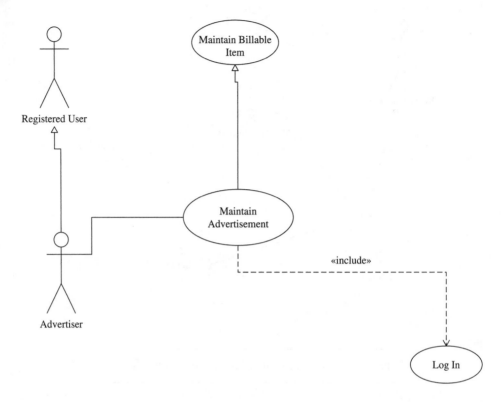

Figure 2-16 An increasingly detailed view of use cases involving advertisers.

Finding the Finish Line

As your use case diagrams and written text documentation are evaluated, you will come up with other ideas and things that you missed. This is to be expected. Document these ideas even if you discard them ultimately. Also be prepared to revise your models as your and your customer's understanding or business climate changes. A growing understanding or a dynamic business climate means more use case diagrams and revisions to existing use case diagrams. If you anticipate the dynamic nature of understanding, then you will have no problem moving on to next steps rather than trying to create a perfect set of use cases up front.

The objective of creating use case diagrams is to document important aspects of the system, to provide users with a low-tech way to visually evaluate your mutual understanding, and then to move on. The outcome we desire is a "good enough," not perfect, set of use cases.

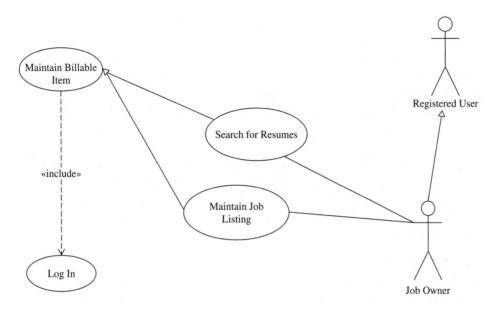

Figure 2-17 This figure shows the relationship between a job owner and his or her use cases, including a clear depiction that authentication is required and that the job owner is managing billable things.

Driving Design with Use Cases

Thus far I have defined significant use cases and use case diagrams for Motown-jobs.com. (I left out "Maintain Customer Information," but I know that I need it.) From the discussion it should be obvious that I left off minor tasks such as reading and writing listings to a database, for example. However, this is covered by "Maintain Job Listing." I don't need a separate use case diagram to show that I am "crudding"—from CRUD, or create, read, update, and delete—listings, advertisements, or résumés, although it will be useful to describe these things in future diagrams such as sequence diagrams (see Chapter 6 for more information). The next thing I am interested in accomplishing is prioritization.

Too many projects skip use cases altogether and ignore prioritization, but use cases exist to help you manage scope and to prioritize. The term *use case–driven design* means that we state what we are building in our use cases to limit scope and avoid wasted time, and we prioritize what we build by starting with the most critical, highest-priority features first. Too often programmers will build cool or easy things such as "About" dialogs first and bells and whistles that aren't needed because they are exploring some new technology, and this is a significant factor in why so many projects fail.

After you have defined your use cases, you will want to prioritize and further design and implement a solution to support those use cases that have the highest priority or represent the most significant risk. How do you decide what to design and build first? The answer is to ask you customer what is most risky, most important, or most valuable and then to focus your energies on those use cases.

NOTE *The real question to ask your customers is: "What features can we build first so that if we run out of time and money, we still will have a marketable product? Customers don't always want to hear the tough questions, and you will have to exercise some diplomacy, but finding the right answer to this question and acting on it may be the most important thing you do.*

For Motown-jobs.com, I decided—as the customer—that I can go to market with a fee-based job listing service. This means that if I implement "Maintain Job Listing," "Search for a Job," and "Maintain Billing Information," I will have a product that I can go to market with. This doesn't mean that I won't build résumé posting, searching, and advertising support into the system—it just means that these aren't the most important features.

Next priorities are tougher. Should I build résumé posting and searching or advertising next? The answer is that I want job seekers to use the service and job owners to see that there is a lot of traffic on and interest in my site, so I will support posting a résumé next—which is a free service but critical—and then résumé searching—which is also a fee service but dependent on having résumés to look through. Finally, I will support advertising, which ultimately is dependent on having enough traffic to interest advertisers.

The important thing here is that identifying my use cases helped me prioritize my list of tasks and illustrates a critical path to my minimal-success criterion—selling help wanted advertisements.

Quiz

1. What symbol represents a use case?

    a. A line

    b. A directed line

    c. A stick figure

    d. An oval containing text

2. An actor can only be a person.

   a. True

   b. False

3. What symbol represents a dependency?

   a. A line

   b. A line with a triangle pointing toward the dependent element

   c. A dashed line with an arrow pointing toward the dependent element

   d. A dashed line with an arrow pointing toward the depended-on element

4. How is a stereotype indicated on a connector?

   a. Text between a pair of guillemots

   b. Plain text next to the connector

   c. The word *stereotype* inside of the oval symbol

5. An inclusion relationship is used for reusing behavior modeled by another user case.

   a. True

   b. False

6. An extension relationship is used for modeling optional system features.

   a. True

   b. False

7. Generalization in the UML is reflected in implementation by

   a. polymorphism.

   b. aggregation.

   c. inheritance.

   d. interfaces.

8. Every capability of a system should be represented by a use case.

   a. True

   b. False

9. In an extend relationship, the arrow points toward the

   a. base use case.

   b. extension use case.

10. It is important to implement the easy use cases first to ensure that early efforts are successful.

    a. True

    b. False

Answers

1. c
2. b
3. d
4. a
5. a
6. a
7. c
8. b
9. a
10. b

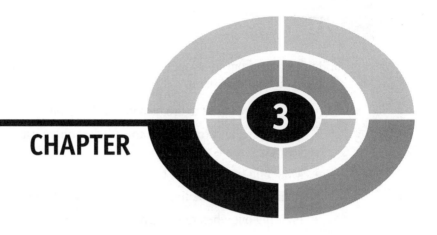

CHAPTER

3

Diagramming Features as Processes

This chapter is about activity diagrams. While my emphasis isn't process, a next step after capturing use cases is to begin describing how the features represented by your use cases will play out. Activity diagrams help you and users to describe visually the sequence of actions that leads you through the completion of a task.

The goal is to converge on code continuously by starting with an understanding of the problem space in general and capturing the problems we will solve—use cases—by describing how those features work and ultimately implementing the solution. Activity diagrams are a useful analysis tool and can be used for process reengineering, i.e., redesigning process. In this way, activity diagrams are a progressive

bridge leading from analysis to design and ultimately to implementation. In this chapter you will learn about

- The symbols used to create activity diagrams
- How to create activity diagrams by describing use cases and scenarios as a series of actions
- Modeling simultaneous behaviors
- Refining physical activities with activity diagrams
- Figuring out when to stop creating activity diagrams

Elaborating on Features as Processes

Few ideas are completely new. Existing concepts are refined and evolve and mature, carrying along some of the old and some of the new. The same is true for analysis and design concepts.

Structured analysis and design emphasized the flowchart. An activity diagram in the Unified Modeling Language (UML) is pretty close to a flowchart. The symbols are similar but not the same. The utility is similar, but there is a difference. Activity diagrams, unlike flowcharts, can model parallel behavior.

Activity diagrams are good analysis diagrams for developers, users, testers, and managers because they use simple symbols, plain text, and a style that is similar to the familiar flowchart. Activity diagrams are good at helping you to capture, visualize, and describe an ordered set of actions from a beginning to an end. Activity diagrams are created as a finite set of serial actions or a combination of serial and parallel actions.

A Journey toward Code

A basic principle of objected-oriented analysis and design is that we want to start from high-level problem-space ideas and concepts and move toward a low-level solution space. The high-level problem space is also referred to as the *problem domain*. The low-level solution space is referred to as the *solution domain*. The UML is a language for capturing and describing our understanding as we move from documenting a problem to coding a solution.

Based on the idea of moving our understanding from concept to design, use cases are a good way to capture the things that describe our problem. For example, we want to match employers to potential employees by providing a job listing board. A use case that supports this is to manage listings. A next step in an abstract sense is to describe how we would go about managing a listing. At this juncture it is still too early to begin talking about databases and programming languages. Instead, we want to talk about the activities that describe our problem, and these activities consist of actions.

NOTE *At an ideological level, analysis and design are processes whereby we decompose a problem into smaller discrete problems so that we can compose small solutions for each discrete problem and ultimately orchestrate the small solutions into a coherent whole. The UML is a language for decomposing a problem and recomposing it as the description of a solution. A language such as Visual Basic.NET is useful for implementing the solution description, and process is how we go about it.*

Understanding Activity Diagram Uses

Activity diagrams are not really about methods or classes. It is still too early for that. The reason that it is too early is because technical things such as polymorphism, inheritance, methods, and attributes generally are meaningless concepts to users and sometimes managers.

Activity diagrams are a means by which we can capture the understanding of people we call *domain experts*. For example, if you are building a jail-management system, then a domain expert might be a corrections officer. A corrections officer probably won't understand the difference between a namespace, class, and interface, but as a designer, you may not understand the significance of a purchase of 50 toothbrushes by an inmate. An activity diagram can help.

A true story—and why consulting can be interesting—is behind the toothbrush metaphor. While working for a large county jail system in Oregon, I had to write a pilot application to demonstrate ASP.NET in its early days. The pilot ultimately would be part of an inmate account-management system for the jail. The basic idea was that prisoners can't be in possession of cash, but they can have money on account to purchase personal items and snacks. The county managed the accounts. Some of the rules included limits on the number of candy bars, say, a diabetic might purchase, as well as a limit on the number of toothbrushes that could be purchased. Not being a corrections officer, it seemed weird to me that anyone would buy more than one toothbrush and weirder still why anyone would care. The problem is that when scraped to a sharp point or split with a piece of a safety razorblade wedged into the split and held in place by a rubber band, a toothbrush can become a formidable weapon. (In reality, I knew this because I either learned it as a military policeman or saw it on an episode of "Oz" on HBO.)

In practice, this story is illustrative of the fact that those on the ground—the domain experts—will know details that you will never think of. Activity diagrams are good for capturing these details in a general sense and in a way that the domain experts can examine, clarify, and improve on.

Working backward from my prisoner account-management story, we might have a use case "Make Purchase" and a scenario in that use case that we need to ensure that the purchase does not violate a safety rule. We can capture this in an activity diagram plainly enough that a corrections officer can tell us if we understand the problem and have decomposed it sufficiently. Figure 3-1 shows an activity diagram for this scenario.

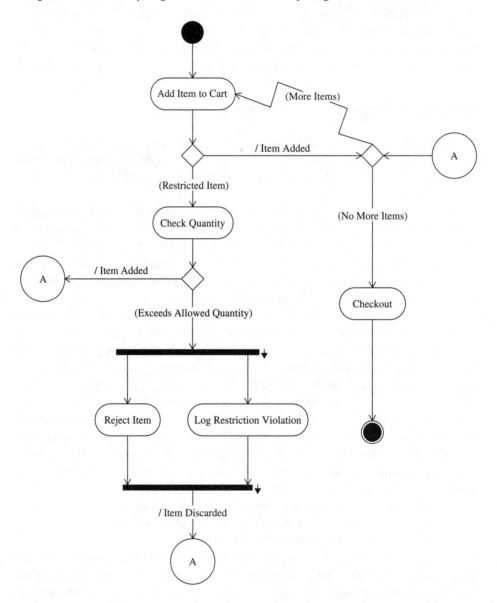

Figure 3-1 An activity diagram that illustrates restrictions on the kind and number of items that can be purchased in prison.

For now, don't worry about what the shapes mean. Simply note the simple text and the flow suggested by the arrows. The general idea is that at a glance—perhaps with a minimum of explanation—this diagram should make sense to users and developers alike. The next section will begin exploring what all these elements and more mean.

Using Activity Diagram Symbols

Activity diagrams can be simple flowcharts that have a finite beginning and ending point or more complex diagrams that model parallel behavior and multiple subflows and define multiple terminuses. I find that diagramming simple activities is an excellent way to get started and that adding too many alternate scenarios in a single diagram makes it both hard to manage and print the diagram and difficult to understand.

Making your activity diagrams comprehensible may be more important than making the diagram comprehensive or all-encompassing. Another mistake is to create activity diagrams for every use case and scenario. Creating diagrams is time-consuming, and a good way to focus your time is by diagramming those aspects that are more critical to solving your problem.

Consider a couple of examples. Programs that store data commonly do so in relational databases. This behavior is called *create, read, update, and delete (CRUD) behavior*. Reading and writing data from a database are so well understood that I wouldn't diagram this behavior as a separate activity. (In fact, the notion of a database really shouldn't show up in an activity diagram.) The entire read-write behavior might be captured at some point in an activity as an action called *fetch and store* or *read and write*. On the other hand—borrowing from Chapter 2—if we are going to expire a customer's job listing and want to give that customer an opportunity to extend the job listing, then this is less common than CRUD behavior, and I would create an activity diagram to explore the sequence of actions. By diagramming the "Expire Listing" activity, I could get the sequence of actions just right, and it might be the catalyst for improving on the quality of service. For example, we might come up with the renew by e-mail feature we discussed in Chapter 2.

If you have created some flowcharts with a tool such as Visio in the past, then activity diagrams will seem pretty straightforward, but keep in mind that activity diagrams can be used to model richer behavior than plain old flowcharts. In order to create activity diagrams, you will need to learn abut the symbols and rules that apply.

TIP *You can think of the symbols and rules of any UML diagram as the* visual grammar *for the language.*

Initial Node

Every activity diagram has one *initial node* symbol. This is a solid circle (see the top of Figure 3-1). You can provide a name and some documentation for the initial node, but generally I do not.

The initial node can have one transition line exiting the node. The transition line is called a *control flow* and is represented by a directed arrow with the arrow pointing away from the initial node. For clarity, just the initial node and a control flow are depicted in Figure 3-2. You can place the initial node anywhere on the diagram you'd like and add the control flow anywhere on the initial node you'd like. Living in the western hemisphere, I have a bias toward upper-left starting points and lower-right ending points.

Control Flow

As mentioned previously, a control flow is a directed arrow. A control flow is also referred to as just a *flow* or an *edge*. The control flow begins at the symbol losing focus and points to and is connected to the thing gaining focus. For example, a control flow might originate at an initial node and terminate at an action, as shown in Figure 3-3.

A common way to adorn a control flow is to add a *guard condition*. A guard condition acts as a sentinel that requires a test be passed before flow continues. In code, commonly this would be implemented as an if-conditional test.

Using Guard Conditions

Without diverting our attention away from guard conditions too much, an *action*— which we will talk about more in the section entitled, "Action"—is something that happens in the flow. An action, like the initial node, is another kind of node. Activity diagrams are wholly composed of various kinds of nodes and flows (or edges).

Figure 3-2 The solid circle is called an *initial node*—or activity diagram starting point—and the directed arrow is called a *control flow*.

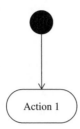

Figure 3-3   An initial node, control flow, and an action.

A guard condition is shown as text in between the left and right square brackets, and you can think of a guard condition as a gatekeeper to the next node (Figure 3-4).

If you have ever served in any kind of militia, then you are familiar with the notion of a password or pass phrase:

> **Guard:** "The sparrow is a harbinger."
>
> **Footsolider:** "Of death, which is the only certainty besides taxes."
>
> **Guard:** "You may pass."

Well, when I was in the army, the pass phrases were never clever, but the idea is the same. The guard represents a test that must be passed to continue. Oddly enough, programmatic tests can be pretty esoteric, but the text you write in your guard conditions will serve your constituency better if they are simple. Figure 3-5 is a practical example of an initial node, an action, and a flow with a guard condition.

In the figure, the initial node transitions to the first action, "Find Customer." The guard condition is that my availability date is known. It doesn't do any good to pile up customers when I have no available time left.

The diagram in Figure 3-5 illustrates how an activity diagram is sort of agnostic when it comes to implementation. The partial activity in Figure 3-5 could be talking about a physical process such as searching the Motown-jobs.com Web site and

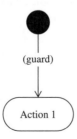

Figure 3-4   An initial node, flow with guard, and a generic action.

(Availability Known)

Find Customer

Figure 3-5 Part of an activity diagram for finding customers.

calling past customers or a software process that automatically scans the Motown-jobs.com Web site through a Web service and e-mails past customers, notifying them of my availability. You will see more instances of guard conditions throughout the examples in this chapter.

Different Ways of Showing Flows

The most common way to diagram a flow is to use a single control flow symbol connecting two nodes, but this isn't the only way. If your diagram is very complex with a lot of overlapping edges, then you can use a connector node (Figure 3-6). An edge can transition from an action to an object to an action (Figure 3-7) and between two pins (Figure 3-8).

Using Connector Nodes

You don't have to use connectors, but if your diagrams become very large or complex, then you will find that your flows begin to overlap or that your activity spans multiple pages. The connector node is a good way to simplify overlapping flows or flows that span multiple pages.

TIP *The version of Visio that I used to create Figure 3-6 does not support the connector node. To create this effect, I had to use the Ellipse tool. The result is that the diagram is visually correct, but Visio will report an error. As is true with many tools, tradeoffs have to be made.*

Figure 3-6 A connector node can be used to simplify busy-looking activity diagrams.

Figure 3-7   Inserting a customer object between two actions related to customers.

To use a connector node, draw a flow exiting a node and transitioning to a connector. Where the connection is made to the next node, draw a connector with a flow exiting the connector and transitioning to the next node in the diagram.

Connector nodes come in pairs. Make sure that connector pairs have the same name; naming connectors will help you to match connection points when you have multiple connector pairs in a single diagram.

Using Objects in Activity Diagrams

Earlier I said that diagramming activities occurs too early in analysis to figure out what the objects are; however, the UML supports adding objects to activity diagrams. After you have had a chance to let users provide you with some feedback and your understanding of the problem space has grown, it may be helpful to add objects to your activity diagrams. The key here is to avoid adding technically complex concepts too early. If you get bogged down in discussions about what an object is or whether the object is named correctly or not, then remove the object. On the other hand, if the object is very obvious—as is depicted in Figure 3-7—and it aids everyone's understanding, then add it.

It is valuable to keep in mind who your constituency is for each kind of diagram. Generally, I think of activity diagrams as analysis tools that end users will read to help you understand how they do their job; explaining object-oriented concepts typically seems to be a distraction, so I leave objects out of activity diagrams.

Using Pins

Pins in the UML are analogous to parameters in implementation. The name or value of a pin leaving one action should be thought of as an input parameter to the next action. Figures 3-7 and 3-8 convey the same information—that there is a customer involved in this flow. Pins, like objects, may be too detailed for everyday use

Figure 3-8   An advanced technique includes connecting two pins on action nodes with a control flow.

and may result in tangential, confusing discussions when working out flows with customers. However, if you are explaining the activities to designers and programmers, then it may be helpful to show objects.

In Figures 3-7 and 3-8 the names of actions—"Find Customer" and "Contact Customer"—clearly suggest that a customer is involved. Leaving out the object and pins—see Figure 3-9—still pretty clearly suggests the participation of a customer without risking lengthy, tangential explanations.

Actions

Action nodes are the things that you do or that happen in an activity diagram, and an edge represents the path you follow to leapfrog from action to action. Action nodes are slightly more rectangular in shape than use case shapes. Two of the most important aspects of actions are the order in which they occur and the name you give them. The name should be short and to the point. Using noun and verb pairs in action names can help you to find classes and methods, but action names are not intended solely for this purpose, and again, it is pretty early in analysis and design to get hung up on implementation details such as classes and methods.

Actions are permitted to have one or more incoming flows and only one outgoing flow. If there is more then one incoming flow, then the action will not transition until all incoming flows have reached that action. Actions can split into alternate paths using the *decision node*—refer to the section entitled, "Decision and Merge Nodes"—or transition into parallel flows using the *fork node*—see the section entitled, "Transition Fork and Transition Merge"—but only a single flow actually should be attached as an outgoing flow for an action.

A good rule of thumb for creating activity diagrams is to describe how a use case begins, progresses, and ends with all the actions that must be completed along the way. Decision and merge nodes and forks and joins are a means of modeling parallel behavior or alternations with the activity itself. If alternate flows are very complex, then you can use the subactivity diagram to compartmentalize the subactivity.

Actions also can use preconditions and postconditions to indicate the necessary conditions before and after an action occurs. Let's chunk these aspects—names,

Figure 3-9   This diagram is simpler than the diagrams showing an object or using pins but still suggests the participation of a customer.

subactivities, and conditions—into subsections to examine how we annotate each aspect of an action.

Naming Actions

I prefer actions to have sufficient detail—a noun and a verb—to describe what happens and what or who is involved, e.g., "Find Customer," "E-mail Customer," "Store Job Listing," "Cancel Listing," and "Delete Résumé." Without a tremendous amount of additional text, these names tell me what the action does and what is acted on. This is important because an essential concept in the UML is that a lot of information is conveyed visually as opposed to with a lot of text.

Ultimately, nouns and verbs will help you to find classes and methods, but it is a good idea to defer thinking about implementation details for a while yet. We simply want to understand how we go about performing an activity but not how we implement that activity.

For example, in Chapter 2 we defined a use case "Manage a Job Listing." This is a use case that arguably consists of several activities, including "Post a Job Listing." Posting a job listing is a scenario in the "Manage a Job Listing" use case, but "Post a Job Listing" is not a single action. There are arguably several actions that would have to be completed to capture the entire activity. Here is a written example that describes posting a job listing, followed by a short activity diagram (Figure 3-10) modeling the same thing:

- Provide job description
- Log-in
- Provide payment information
- Process payment
- Store job description
- Provide confirmation

Once we have an initial diagram—shown in Figure 3-10—we have a good basis for holding a discussion about the activity. We can bring in domain experts and ask them about details of the activity diagram and evaluate this information to determine if we need to revise the diagram. For instance, we may want to check if valid payment information on file can be used or we want new payment information. Or if the user is a new user, then we may need to add a decision point that permits the user to register and then log in.

A real implicit benefit here is that a reasonable stab at an activity diagram captures the modeler's understanding and permits others to provide feedback and elaborate on the flow, adding or removing detail as necessary.

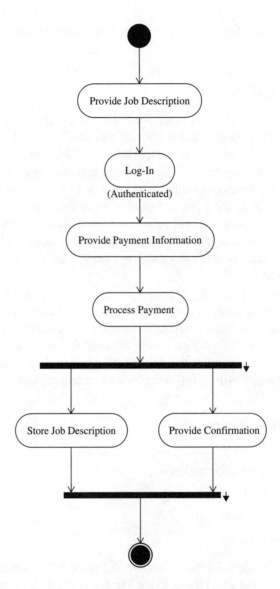

Figure 3-10 A model showing the actions required to post a job.

Adding Preconditions and Postconditions

Preconditions and postconditions can be added to a model using a note—the stereotype symbols with the word *precondition* or the word *postcondition* in between and the name of the condition. The note is attached to the action to which the condition or conditions applies. This is referred to as *design by contract* and often is implemented

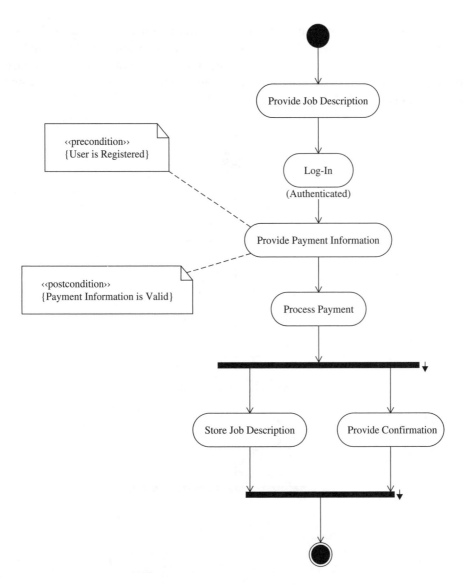

Figure 3-11   Using a precondition and postcondition constraint.

in code as an assertion combined with a conditional test. Figure 3-11 shows a precondition and postcondition applied to the "Provide Payment Information" action.

In Figure 3-11, the diagram requires the precondition that the user is registered and the postcondition that the payment information is valid. As is true with code, there is more than one way to represent this information. For example, we could use a guard condition before and after the "Provide Payment Information" action (Figure 3-12), or we could use a decision node (see "Decision and Merge Nodes") to branch to a register action before permitting payment information to be provided, and we could have an action to validate payment information after the payment information is provided (Figure 3-13).

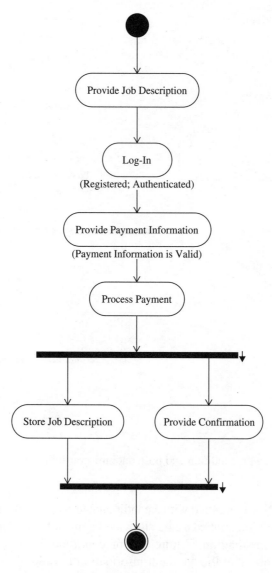

Figure 3-12   Using guards to express a precondition and a postcondition.

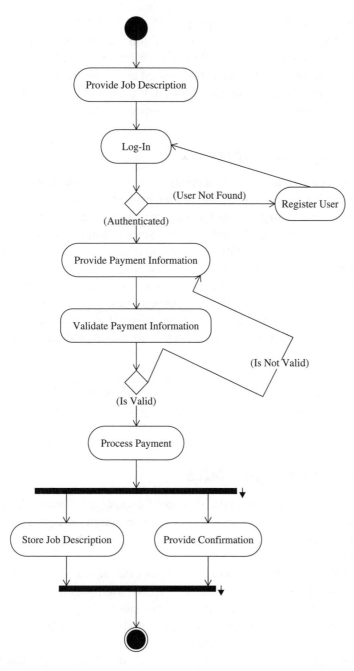

Figure 3-13   Using a decision node to indicate that users must register and provide valid payment information.

All three of these diagrams—Figures 3-11, 3-12, and 3-13—convey the same information. The real difference is stylistic. If you want the diagram to appear less busy, try using the guard condition. If the constraint style—in Figure 3-11—seems more meaningful, then use that style. If you want to explore registration and address validation, then use the decision node styles in Figure 3-13. In that figure, the decision nodes are represented by the diamond-shaped symbols.

Modeling Subactivities

Sometimes it is easy to add too much detail to a single activity diagram, making the diagram busy and confusing. For example, if we expand "Register User" in Figure 3-13 to include all the necessary actions for registering users, such as obtaining a unique user name and password and validating and storing mailing address information, then the main focus of the activity—creating and paying for a job listing—may be lost in the noise of all the additional actions and edges.

If in any instance we find the details of subactivities making a diagram too confusing, or we find that we want to reuse subactivities, then we can mark an action as a subactivity with a fork inside the action. (Visio doesn't support the subsidiary activity symbol, so I drew one from scratch in Microsoft Paint and added it to the "Register User" action in Figure 3-13.)

TIP *If you want to invent or find that an aspect of the UML isn't supported by your specific modeling tool, then consider using a stereotype or a note to document your meaning.*

Decision and Merge Nodes

Decision and merge nodes were called *decision diamonds* in flowcharts. This diamond-shaped symbol is one of the elements that makes an activity diagram reminiscent of a flowchart. Decision and merge nodes use the same symbol and convey conditional branching and merging.

When the diamond-shaped symbol is used as a *decision node*—after "Log-In" in Figure 3-13—it has one edge entering the node and multiple edges exiting the node. When used as a *merge node*, there are multiple entering edges and a single exiting edge. A decision node takes only one exit path, and a merge node doesn't exit until all flows have arrived at the merge node.

The guard conditions on a decision node act like if..else logic and should be mutually exclusive, which necessarily implies that if one guard condition is met, then the other must fail. As depicted in Figure 3-13, you can stipulate both guard conditions literally or stipulate one guard condition and use an [Else] guard for the alternate condition.

A merge node marks the end of conditional behavior started by a decision node. We don't need a merge node in Figure 3-13 because we rerouted the newly registered user back to the "Log-In" action. However, if we wanted to be a little nicer, we might simply authenticate the new user automatically and proceed right to providing payment information where he or she left off. This revision is shown using a merge node in Figure 3-14. (Note that the guard conditions for the decision node following the "Log-In" action were modified to show the use of the [Else] guard style.)

Transition Forks and Joins

A *fork* exists to depict parallel behavior, and a *join* is used to converge parallel behavior back into a single flow. Forked behavior does not specify whether or not the behavior is interleaved or occurs simultaneously; the implication is simply that the forked actions are occurring during a shared, concurrent interval. Usually forked behavior is implemented as multithreaded behavior. (Figure 3-13 presents an example of a fork after the "Process Payment" action and a join immediately before the final node.)

When multiple flows enter an action, this is implicitly a join, and the meaning is that the outgoing flow occurs *only* when all incoming flows have reached the action. Your diagrams will be clearer if you use forks and joins explicitly where you mean to show parallel behavior.

In Figure 3-13 we mean that we can store a job description and provide the user with a confirmation simultaneously or concurrently but that both these things must occur before the activity is considered complete.

Partitioning Responsibility with Swimlanes

Sometimes you want to show who or what is responsible for part of an activity. You can do this with *swimlanes*. Modeling tools typically show swimlanes as a box with a name at the top, and you place whatever nodes and edges that belong to that thing in that swimlane. You can have as many swimlanes as it makes sense to have, but boxy swimlanes can make it hard to organize your activity diagram.

UML version 2.0 supports vertical, horizontal, and gridlike partitions, so the swimlane metaphor is no longer precise. The actual terminology is now *activity partition*, but the word *swimlane* is still employed in general conversation and used in modeling tools.

Using Swimlanes

If we want to show who or what is responsible for various actions in Figure 3-14, then we can add a swimlane (or partition) for what we believe the partitions to be.

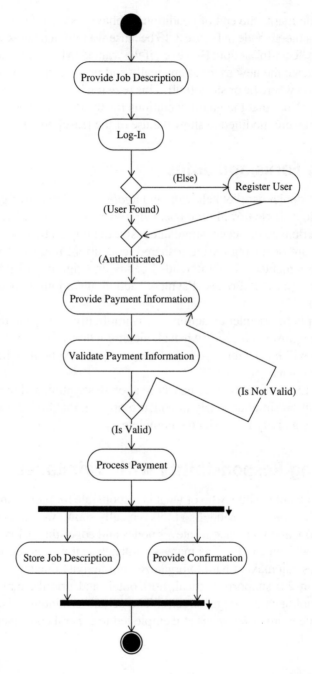

Figure 3-14 A merge node used to converge when a branch is taken after a new user registers.

In the example, we could say that posting a job is divided into two partitions, the user and the system, and add a swimlane for each partition (Figure 3-15). If we decided that payment processing represents a distinct partition, then we could add a third partition and move the process payment action into that partition (Figure 3-16).

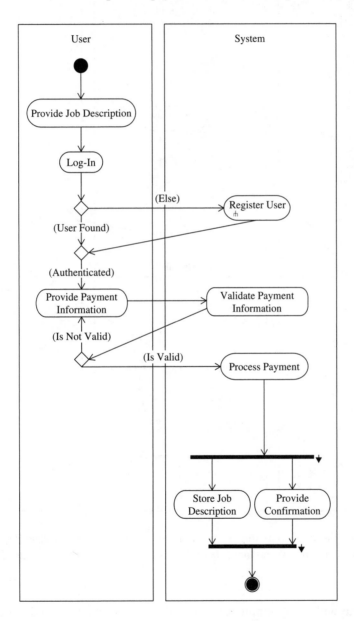

Figure 3-15   Actions are divided between a user and the system.

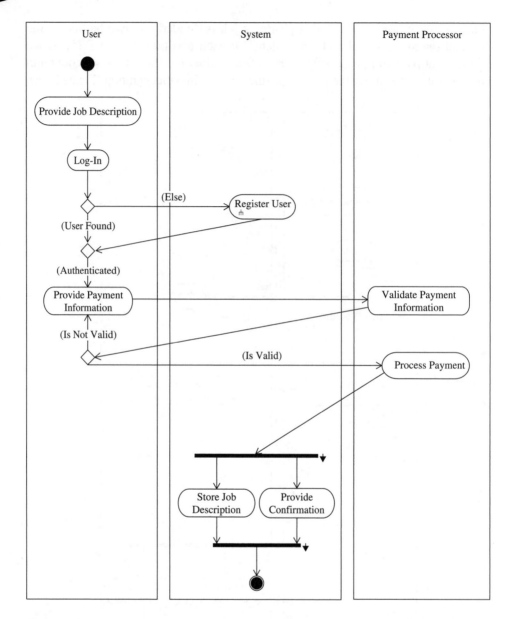

Figure 3-16 Further subdividing responsibilities by placing the "Validate Payment Information" and "Process Payment" actions in a separate partition called the "Payment Processor."

As is true with programming, you can divide your analysis and design into as many partitions as you want. There are tradeoffs for adding partitions in models just as there are tradeoffs for adding partitions in code. Partitioning models may help you to organize, but all those partitions suggest partitioned software that will have to be orchestrated and reassembled to accomplish the goals of the system.

Modeling Actions that Spans Partitions

Sometimes an action may belong to more than one partition at a time. For example, "Register User" really doesn't belong to the user or the system. We know from earlier discussions that "Register User" is a subsidiary activity that may involve the user providing personal information and the system validating address information and storing the user information. However, the UML doesn't permit a node to span more than one partition in a single dimension. As a result, you will have to pick a partition for the node, and this also suggests what we know to be true about "Register User"—that it can be decomposed into its own activity.

Using Multidimensional Partitions

Modeling multidimensional activity partitions is a relatively new concept. Diagramming multidimensional activity partitions also doesn't seem to be wholly supported by some popular and currently available modeling tools; however, you can simulate a multidimensional partition in Visio by adding two swimlanes (activity partitions) and rotating one of them. (The result is a diagram similar to Figure 3-17.) Now that we have the mechanics for creating a multidimensional partition, you might be wondering how it is used.

An action in an activity partition matrix belongs wholly to both partitions. Suppose, for example, that as we are gearing up to sell job listings on Motown-jobs .com, we decide to use PayPal to process payments. We can say that "Process Payment" is part of both our "Payment Processor" and PayPal's payment-processing system, which is reflected in Figure 3-17.

Indicating Timed Signals

Thus far we haven't talked about when things occur. There are three types of signals that facilitate talking about time in activity diagrams. These are the *time signal*, the *send signal*, and the *accept signal*. A signal indicates that an outside event has fired, and that event initiates the activity.

The hourglass shape of the time signal is used to specify an interval of time. For example, we could use the time signal to indicate that the "Expire Listing" activity will start after the listing has been available for 30 days (Figure 3-18). The receive

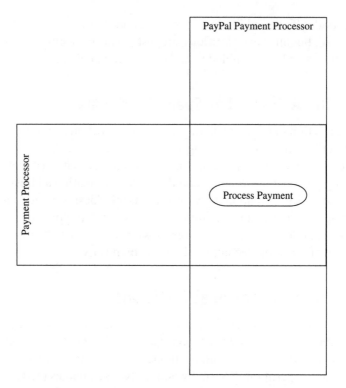

Figure 3-17 Multidimensional partitions, where an action is owned by two partitions in different dimensions at the same time.

signal symbol is a rectangle with a wedge cut into it, and the send signal symbol is a rectangle with a protruding wedge—making the receive and send signal symbols look a bit like jigsaw puzzle pieces (again shown in Figure 3-18).

Note *Every tool has its limitations. In Visio, for example, there is no symbol for a time signal, so I contrived one, and the send and receive signals are used as an alternative form of documenting events. Visio's implementation isn't precisely consistent with the UML; it is important not to get hung up on these little inconsistencies that you are bound to run into. Rather than spending your time drawing pictures for unsupported aspects of the UML, try using a note instead.*

The model in Figure 3-18 is understood to mean that 30 days after a listing is posted, it will be expired automatically unless a notified owner elects to extend it. Alternate signals include a user deleting a listing, which causes the listing to be

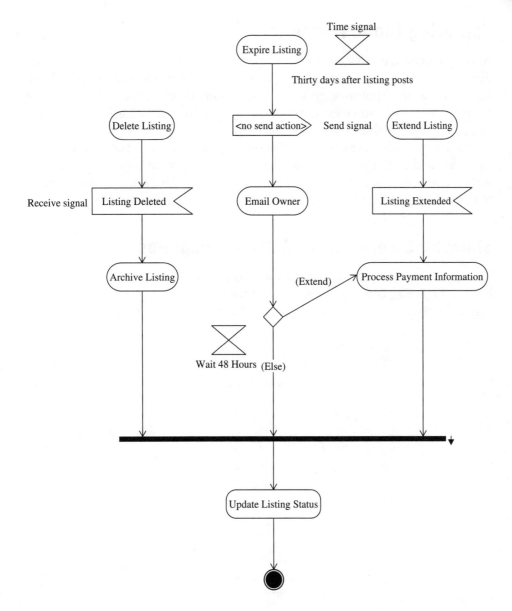

Figure 3-18   A time signal for expiring a listing, two receive signals for extending and deleting a listing, and a send signal for notifying a listing about an impending expiration.

archived before being delisted and an owner taking his or her own initiative to extend the listing prior to its expiration. If the owner extends the listing, then this signals the system to process an additional payment.

Capturing Input Parameters

Activity diagrams can have input parameters, e.g., in Figure 3-18 in every instance that we are talking about doing something with a listing. We could show a "Listing" object as the input for each action in the figure. Grabbing just a small piece of Figure 3-18, we can show the notation and symbol for indicating that the input to that action is a "Listing" object (Figure 3-19).

While input objects can be useful for developers, this is another instance where they may add confusion to the discussion of the activity in a general, analytical sense. At least during early phases of analysis, consider deferring specific reference to implementation details such as classes.

Showing Exceptions in Activity Diagrams

The UML supports modeling *exceptions*. An exception is shown as a zigzagging line (or "lightning bolt") with the name of the class of the exception adorning the zigzagging line. The exception handler can be modeled as an action node with the

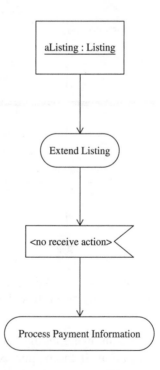

Figure 3-19 The "Listing" object is shown as an input parameter to the "Extend Listing" action and its containing activity diagram.

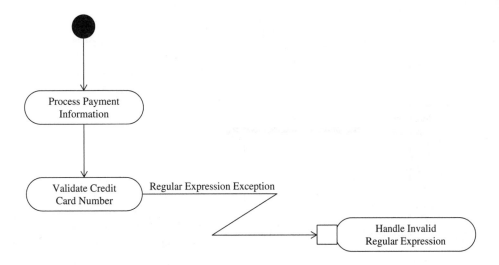

Figure 3-20   Modeling an exception in an activity diagram.

name of the action in the node and the exception flow connecting to an input pin on
the exception action node (Figure 3-20).

The node containing the exception handler has no return flow. An exception handler just hangs off the action that caused the error to occur. It is important to
remember that we are capturing general flow and actions; during this phase, we do
not have to indicate how we are handling the exception.

Concepts such as exception, exception handler, stack unwinding, and performance may add considerably to the confusion for nontechnical users. If you can
add an exception and exception action node without getting bogged down in discussions about how exception handlers are implemented or how they work, then go
ahead and add them to your activity diagrams.

Terminating Activity Diagrams

When you reach the end of an activity, add an *activity final node.* If you reach the end
of a flow and nothing else happens, add a *flow final node* (Figure 3-21). You can have
more than one activity final node and flow final node in a single activity diagram.

The activity diagram in Figure 3-21 shows that we process all the expired listings
until there are no more, and for each expired listing, we e-mail the owner, providing
him or her with an opportunity to renew the listing or let it expire. Notice that when
the decision node branches because there are no more expired listings, it simply

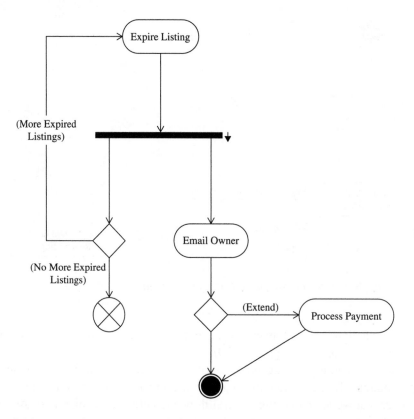

Figure 3-21   An activity showing a flow final node and an activity final node.

dead ends. You might envision this sort of activity implemented as an asynchronous process where each expired listing fires off a process to permit the listing owner to renew the listing.

Creating Activity Diagrams

A decision as important as what goes into an activity diagram is what to diagram. Too often it is easy to keep adding additional models and adding more detail to existing models. The implication, though, is that while you are modeling, someone else is waiting to implement your design, or worse, while you are refining your designs, some poor implementer will have to modify their implementation. For this reason, it is important to make your activity diagrams relatively simple; limit the activity diagrams you create to important, critical, or challenging aspects of your problem; and avoid trying to make them perfect. A good model that is easy to understand and completed in a timely matter is more valuable than a perfect model later—if there is such a thing as a perfect model.

Examples of the activity diagrams I would create for use cases from Chapter 2 might be an activity for "Manage Job Listing," "Expire Listing," and "Maintain Billing Information." Specifically, I am interested in understanding the critical aspects of the system, especially those for services that are billable items. Common things such as searching or logging are understood well enough that it is unlikely that I would create an activity diagram for them.

Picking what to model and what not to model is a lot like adding salt during cooking: You can always add a little more, but it is hard to remove salt if you have added too much. The same is true with modeling: You cannot recoup time spent modeling obvious activities, but you always can add more activity diagrams later if you need to.

Reengineering Process

Probably the most beneficial use of activity diagrams is to help nondomain personnel—usually the technologists who will implement a solution—understand a domain. Implicit in the preceding statement is that while domain experts and technologists are attempting to reach a common understanding, there is an opportunity to reengineer the process. Let's take a moment to review what is meant by *process reengineering*.

Frequently, people do there jobs every day without ever identifying a formal process. The process knowledge is known only to the practitioners. Often these same organizations are shocked to discover how much overhead and waste exist within their organization. Process reengineering is a kind of pseudoscience that entails first documenting an organization's processes and then looking for ways to optimize those processes.

I am not an expert in process reengineering, but there are historical examples where well-known companies have spent a considerable amount of money and energy to refine their business processes, and the results have led to broad, sweeping changes in industry. An interesting example can be found in *Behind the Golden Arches*, which details the evolutionary path that led McDonald's to use centralized distribution centers for its franchisees.

NOTE *Ironically enough, software development itself is an example of a domain where the practitioners have defined the process in an ad hoc way. Many software companies are now beginning to realize that they are long overdue for an introspective examination of the processes they follow to build software. Has anyone in your organization every used an activity diagram (or flowchart) to document how your organization builds software?*

Software development is a business of automating solutions to problems. In a general sense it is a useful idea to document critical domain processes and explore some possible optimizations before writing code. If the process is simplified, then the ensuing implementation may be markedly simplified too.

Reengineering a Subactivity

Here is an example involving a subactivity called "Interior Cabin Check" that has to do with the preflight inspection of a small airplane. The idea behind the interior cabin check is that we are looking for required or important things in the interior of the airplane and performing steps to help with some exterior checks. There is a very good likelihood that if we miss something, then we could be taking off with unsafe conditions or not have critical resources during an emergency. (If it bothers you that this doesn't sound like a software problem, then just imagine that we are documenting this problem to write testing or simulation software.)

One of the planes I fly is a Cessna 172 Skyhawk. The interior cabin check (depicted in Figure 3-22) consists of

- Making sure the ignition switch is off
- Turning the master switch on so that we have power
- Lowering the flaps
- Checking for the registration, airworthiness certificate, weight and balance information, and operating handbook, which includes emergency procedures
- Checking the fuel level indicators and fuel selector
- Turning the master switch off

As shown in the activity diagram in Figure 3-22, the steps are carried out consecutively. (This is the way that I performed the inspection the first couple of times I performed it.) An experienced pilot (a domain expert) will tell you that it takes

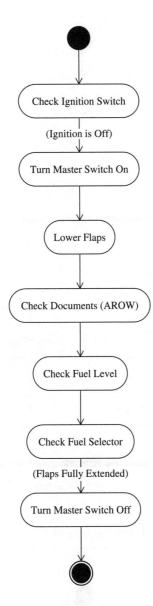

Figure 3-22   Our initial understating is that each task in the activity is performed consecutively.

a few moments for the flaps to come down, so some of the other checks can be performed concurrently. We can tighten up the activity diagram as shown in Figure 3-23.

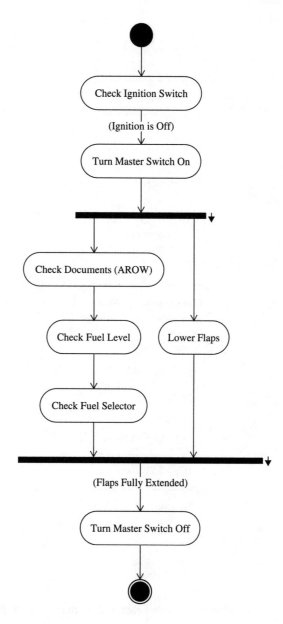

Figure 3-23   Making some tasks concurrent will improve the time to completion of the activity.

Knowing When to Quit

Applying rules consistently will help you to work efficiently during the modeling phase of development. With this in mind, recall that I said that an important idea is to capture the most critical use cases and tackle those first. The same is true of activity diagrams. Identify the use cases that are most critical, and create activity diagrams for those use cases that require some exploration. For instance, authenticating a user in Motown-jobs.com is necessary, but this is a well-understood problem. I wouldn't spend a lot of time creating an activity diagram for this, and I wouldn't work on that activity diagram before I worked on those related to my primary use case, "Manage Job Listing."

If you are not sure how many activity diagrams to create, then try creating an activity diagram for each of the primary functions of your most important use cases. Try to get as much about the activity modeled as quickly and as accurately as you can. Immediately check back with your domain experts, and explore the activities to see if you have captured the most salient points.

Finally, don't permit yourself to get bogged down here. If you can't reach a consensus on the completeness of a particular activity, then set it aside and agree to come back to it. There may be other elements of the problem that will increase your understanding or your users' understanding of the problem in general and resolve the problem you set aside. The key is not to get stuck on any particular problem too early.

Quiz

1. Synonyms for a transition are
    a. connector and flow.
    b. edge and flow.
    c. edge and connector.
    d. action and event.
2. In general, activity diagrams consist of
    a. nodes and edges.
    b. actions and transitions.
    c. actions, decisions, and flows.
    d. symbols and lines.

3. An exception can be shown in an activity diagram with a lightning bolt–shaped edge.

   a. True

   b. False

4. A decision node and merge node use

   a. different symbols.

   b. identical symbols.

   c. either identical or differing symbols depending on context.

5. Multiple flows entering an action node constitute

   a. an implicit merge.

   b. an implicit join.

6. Every flow waits at a merge and join until all flows have arrived.

   a. True

   b. False

7. The swimlane metaphor is no longer used

   a. because swimlanes are no longer part of the UML.

   b. because partitions can be multidimensional and don't look like swimlanes.

   c. The swimlane metaphor is still in use.

   d. Both b and c.

8. Actions can exist in two activity partitions in different dimension at the same time.

   a. True

   b. False

9. A decision and merge node is represented by

   a. an oval.

   b. a circle.

   c. a rectangle.

   d. a diamond.

10. Activity diagrams differ from flowcharts because activity diagrams support
    a. swimlanes.
    b. parallel behavior.
    c. decision nodes.
    d. actions.

Answers

1. b
2. a
3. a
4. b
5. b
6. a
7. d
8. a
9. d
10. b

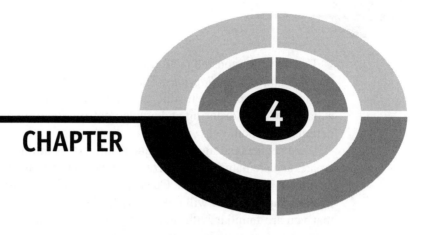

Discovering Behaviors with Interaction Diagrams

Demystify means to "expose, set straight, or throw light on," and each chapter does this implicitly or explicitly. In this chapter I'd like to start off by setting you straight right away. There are all kinds of Unified Modeling Language (UML) diagrams. Some are redundant, and you definitely do not have to create every kind of diagram to have a good design. There is more than one kind of interaction diagram, and the rule of avoiding redundancy is apropos to this chapter.

The two common interaction diagrams are the *sequence* and the *collaboration* (or *communication*) *diagrams.* These diagrams tell you exactly the same thing. Sequences have an explicit time ordering and are linear, and collaborations have a "labeled" time ordering and are geometric. You only need one or the other, but definitely not both.

I like sequence diagrams. Sequence diagrams are more common, very easy to create, and are naturally organized, and we don't need to indicate the time ordering by annotating the messages. Consequently, in this chapter I will emphasize the sequence diagram, but I will talk briefly (and demonstrate) collaboration diagrams so that you are familiar with them. (If you decide ultimately you like the geometric organization of collaboration diagrams, then use those. Remember, though, that you don't need both sequences and collaborations, and many UML tools will readily convert sequences to collaborations and vice versa automatically.)

In this chapter I will show you how to

- Identify the elements of sequence diagrams
- Create sequence and collaboration diagrams
- Understand the time ordering of interaction diagrams
- Use interaction diagrams to discover classes and methods
- Model success and failure scenarios using interaction frames introduced in UML version 2.0
- Use sequences to explore the behavior of many objects across a use case

Elements of Sequence Diagrams

Every diagram uses only a subset of the tokens and grammar that make up the UML. Learning about those tokens and the specific grammar is an essential evil. It is important to remember that you don't need to remember every word in a language to communicate effectively—for example, I can't remember what *solecism* means precisely, as in "for it is the solecism of a prince to think to control the end yet not endure the mean"—but it is important to master a language to employ it creatively.

NOTE *It is important to remember that the UML is an evolving language. As with spoken languages, effective communication can occur with a very basic understanding of the language. The key is to remember to leave the language lawyering to others. (In this case, leave the language lawyering to the Object Management Group.)*

Let's take a couple of minutes to explore the useful tokens and grammar of sequence diagrams. We will begin with the two basic and essential elements of sequence diagrams—lifelines and messages. (It is worthwhile to note that a passable dialogue can occur with just these two elements of sequence diagrams.)

Using Object Lifelines

A *lifeline* is a rectangle with a vertical line descending from the rectangle. The lifeline represents an instance of a class, and the vertically descending line is a convenient place to attach incoming and outgoing messages. Adding multiple lifelines to a single diagram and attaching these with time-ordered messages permits you to show all the classes and messages necessary to complete a scenario described by a use case. By eliminating ambiguous gaps or avoiding the repetition of classes and messages, you can get a whole solution, one scenario at a time.

An object lifeline takes form as an object that plays a part of a role in a use case. I'll talk more about lifelines as we progress; for now, just look at the symbol in Figure 4-1.

Object lifelines can represent actors or objects. Both actors and objects may or may not be actualized as code. This may sound confusing, but it is not. Suppose, for example, that we are building an airline ticketing reservation system. An actor might be a person working the counter in the terminal or a kiosk (used for e-tickets). The person is an important participant in the ticketing sequence but will not be represented by code. A kiosk is also an important participant, and it will be represented by code to some extent. Thus we can refer to an actor called a "Ticketing Authority" and mean both the person and the kiosk.

In some modeling tools, the stick-figure actor is used with an attached lifeline, and in others, a box with a stick figure or <<actor>> stereotype is used. More important

Figure 4-1   An object lifeline represents an instance of a class and a line conveniently placed to permit connecting objects by messages.

than the precise notation is to remember that an actor may or may not be realized in code and that a lifeline can be an actor.

A lifeline also can represent an actualized class. What is important to know is that a lifeline is generally a *noun* that may or may not be codified as a class but is definitely something that can interact with your system and that a lifeline is also just a rectangle with a vertical line descending from it.

Activating a Lifeline

Objects have a lifetime. For example, in a deterministic language such as C++, an object lives until the destructor is called. In a nondeterministic language such as C# (pronounced "C sharp"), an object lives until it is garbage collected. This means that the programmer doesn't really know when the object goes away. However, modelers are not entirely constrained by the implementation language.

From our perspective, we only care when we begin using an object and when we are done using an object unless the object represents a finite resource. In both cases, the activation line represents the span of an object's lifetime for practical purposes. It is also important to know that an object can be represented as being created and destroyed using a single lifeline.

The activation symbol is a vertical rectangle replacing the lifeline for the duration of that instance's existence (Figure 4-2), keeping in mind that an object can be created and destroyed multiple times and that one lifeline is used to represent all

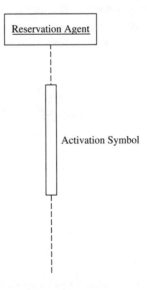

Figure 4-2   A lifeline with an annotated activation symbol.

instances of that class in a sequence. (I will talk about deterministic destruction in a minute.) If we want to express nested or recursive messages, then we can stack activation symbols horizontally.

Sending Messages

Messages are directed lines connecting lifelines. The line begins at one lifeline, and the arrow points toward a lifeline containing the message invoked. The message can begin and end on the same lifeline; this is a *nested call*. A filled-in triangle represents a synchronous message. A stick triangle represents an asynchronous message, and a dashed line is used for return messages. Included as possible messages are found messages and lost messages. A found message is a message with a known receiver, but the sender is not known, and a lost message has a known sender but no specified receiver. Figure 4-3 shows each type of message clearly labeled.

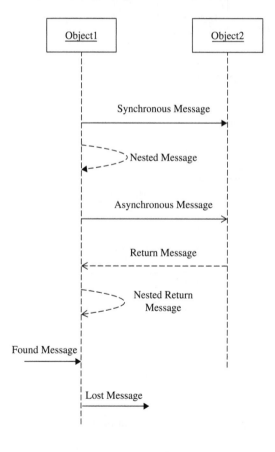

Figure 4-3 Synchronous and asynchronous method call symbols.

We also can specify deterministic object deconstruction by adding a circle with an X in it at the message origin. For languages such as Visual Basic.NET and Java, deterministic object deletion is not supported, but a language such as C++ requires it. (You are likely to seldom encounter a deletion message unless it is critical that you remind developers to free finite resources.)

Suppose that we want to use a specific authentication and authorization scheme in Motown-jobs.com. We could create a sequence that describes how we want to implement the "Log In" use case. Look at the sequence in Figure 4-4 and see if you can follow along. A description of the sequence follows the figure.

The user object uses the actor stereotype. (You could use an actor symbol, too.) The user will not be realized as code but participates in the sequence. Beginning from top left and working our way to the bottom right, we set the user name and password and then send the message "LogIn." (This is interpreted as the "Log-In"

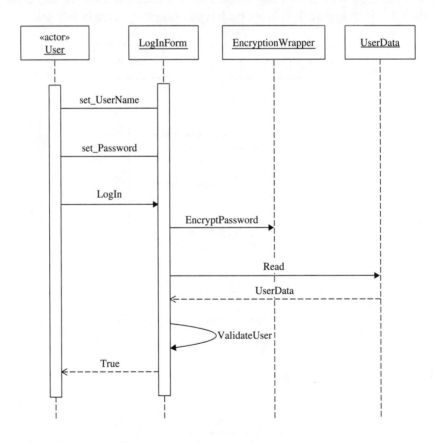

Figure 4-4   A sequence diagram for authenticating a user.

form having a method named "LogIn.") Next, the user-supplied password is encrypted and compared with the encrypted password stored as part of the UserData. If ValidateUser succeeds, then we return a Boolean message true.

The sequence diagram is good at showing us how objects are orchestrated and used across a use case, but they aren't good at showing us how this behavior is implemented. For example, we could use Secure Hash Algorithm 1 (SHA1) encryption with a salt and store the user data with an encrypted password, but the sequence doesn't make this clear. (For a resolution as to how to implement a sequence, refer to the section entitled, "Understanding What Sequences Tell Us.")

Adding Constraints and Notes

You can add notes and constraints to help disambiguate the meaning of particular aspects of your sequence diagrams. The UML describes how these elements are added, but in practice, they vary some depending on the tool you use. For example, we could add a note to the diagram in Figure 4-4 that indicates that we are using SHA1 and a salt value and storing the password in an encrypted form only (Figure 4-5).

Constraints can be added as plain text, pseudocode, actual code, or Object Constraint Language (OCL). Actual code or OCL constraints can be used to help code-generating UML tools generate lines of code. In some heavyweight modeling processes, the ability to generate code may be a requirement, but to date, it seems harder to create UML models that generate granular code than it is to write the code itself. You will have to decide for yourself if you need moderately detailed or very detailed models.

TIP *Models that generate complete applications are unrealistic and impractical. Avoid falling into the trap of trying to create perfect models with enough detail to spit out an application.*

Using Interaction Frames

Interaction frames (or *combined fragments*) are new in UML version 2.0. Interaction frames are rectangular regions used to organize interaction diagrams (sequence and timing diagrams). Interaction frames can surround an entire interaction diagram or just part of a diagram. Each interaction frame is tagged with a specific word (or an abbreviated form of that word), and each kind of interaction frame conveys some specific information. Table 4-1 defines the current interaction frame types.

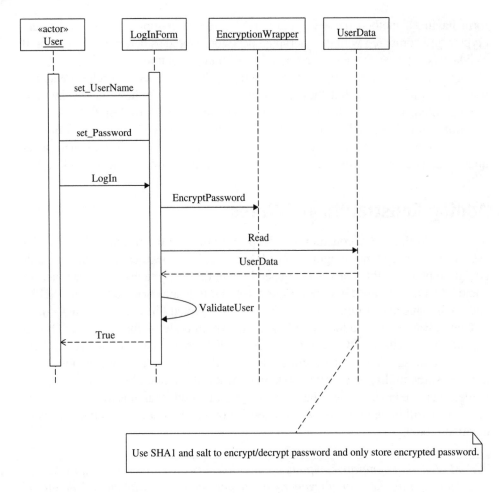

Figure 4-5   Using notes to add detail to your sequence diagrams.

Alt	Alternatives fragments (i.e., conditional logic); only guard conditions evaluating to true will execute.
Loop	The guard indicates how many times this part will execute.
Neg	An invalid interaction.
Opt	Equivalent to an alt with one condition (i.e., an if condition with no else statement).
Par	Fragments are run in parallel—think multithreading.
Ref	Reference to an interaction defined on another diagram.
Region	Critical region; think not reentrant or only one thread at a time.
Sd	Used to surround an entire sequence diagram, if desired.

Table 4-1   The Types of Interaction Frames

The UML is meant to be extensible. If you think of another kind of frame, then use it, as long as you define it. Deviating from the standardized UML is done all the time; this is consistent with how all languages evolve. There are examples of slang that get adopted in spoken languages all the time.

Let's spend a few minutes looking at interaction frames. The key to using interaction frames is to pick the frame type you need, specify the guard conditions that determine how the interaction in the frame is executed, and add the correct number of fragments (or frame divisions). Let's start with the loop frame. This is basically a for.. next, for..each, or while construct as it might appear in a UML model (Figure 4-6).

Note *Earlier in this book I said that I would use Visio to demonstrate that you didn't have to spend thousands of dollars to create usable UML models. Figure 4-6 demonstrates that we can create new UML version 2.0 elements—e.g., loop interaction frame—even though these aren't supported directly by Visio. (The interaction in the figure was created with the simple line drawing tools in Visio.) In the case of interaction frames, I haven't seen any current UML tools that support this construct. The current version of Rational for XDE and Visio doesn't include interaction frames. You can check Togethersoft's offerings and Poseidon for UML.*

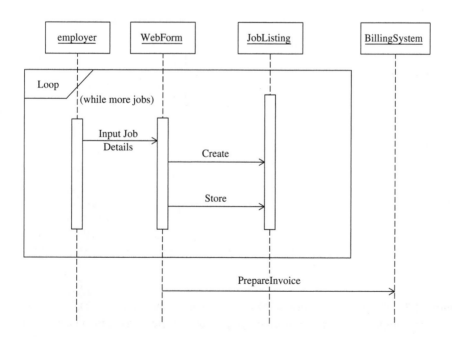

Figure 4-6 An interaction frame showing the loop frame; we are looping through the creation of multiple job listings.

We read the sequence diagram the same as before, except that all the messages in the loop frame are part of the repeating behavior that this sequence describes. (An older-style notation was to use an asterisk as a guard condition. The same model using the multiplicity symbol (an asterisk) is shown in Figure 4-7.)

The key to successful modeling is to remember that it happens in a world with real constraints—budget for tools, available time, the tool's compatibility, the current definition of the UML, and so on. Don't get hung up language lawyering. If your tool doesn't support a particular construct, fudge. In practice, I would not take the time to manually draw an interaction frame if my tool didn't support it; I'd use the asterisk guard condition.

Figure 4-8 shows another common interaction frame, the *alternative frame.* Suppose that we offer perquisites for customers who frequently post a certain number of jobs. We may want to pass these customers to a different billing system, perhaps offering a special volume discount.

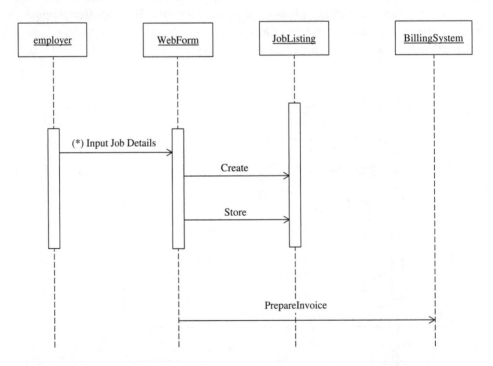

Figure 4-7   The guard condition—[*]—by the name of the "Input Job Details" message indicates multiplicity or repetition, employing an older style devised to indicate a loop.

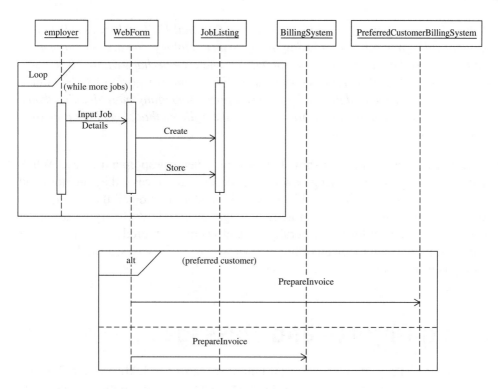

Figure 4-8   An example of an alternative interaction frame.

Understanding What Sequences Tell Us

Older-style sequence diagrams had a singular nature, but with interaction frames we can more conveniently convey behavioral alternatives, parallel behavior, and loops and clearly reference-related sequences. Implicit in the top-left to bottom-right ordering of sequence diagrams is a time ordering that shows how a single use case is supported by multiple objects.

Sequences do not have to be complex to be useful. Most important are the objects across the horizontal and each object's lifeline and the order and name of the messages sent between objects. You do have the option of staggering the lifelines, creating a jagged effect; occasionally you will see this style of sequence. Staggered or horizontally aligned, the meaning is the same.

Note A complete model is subjective. In the Rational Unified Process (RUP), more detail is preferable. Employing the Agile methodology, you are encouraged to create models that are barely good enough. Ultimately—perhaps within 50 years— software models will be required to be as detailed and as rigorous as electronic wiring diagrams, but that day isn't here yet. I prefer something more detailed than the barely good enough models prescribed by the Agile methodology but never so much as to generate lines of code.

Use sequence diagrams to show how several objects prop up a use case. While sequences are good at showing how objects occur in a use case, they are not good at describing specific behavior. If you want to model more detail than a sequence supports, then consider using an activity diagram or code itself; trying to model code at the statement level is generally more efficiently captured simply by writing the code. If you want to see an orthogonal view—many use cases, a single object— then you want a statechart (see Chapter 8).

Discovering Objects and Messages

Use cases should contain success and failure scenarios. In UML version 2.0, you can use the alternation construct to show what happens when things are going as planned and what to do when things go haywire.

Sequence diagrams are also good at helping you to discover classes and methods. The classes can be identified easily as a noun name for the instance of your objects, and methods are the messages that are invoked on an object. It may not be immediately evident what the parameters for these methods are, but classes and methods are a good start.

Owing to the sequential nature of sequences, they also can be good at helping you to identify gaps. For instance, suppose that you discover that a sequence has a lot of notes to explain what is happening. This may indicate that there needs to be some well-named objects and messages that define the annotated behavior. (Generally, I find that well-named classes and methods in code are preferable to comments that try to clarify long methods and well-named objects, and messages in models are preferable to a lot of notes.) Let the sequence be self-explanatory to the extent possible. Consider Figure 4-9, which shows a possible design for the search behavior for Motown-jobs.com.

In the figure we have a job seeker, a search page, and something called a *search engine*. This design doesn't tell us the form of the search criteria or whether we

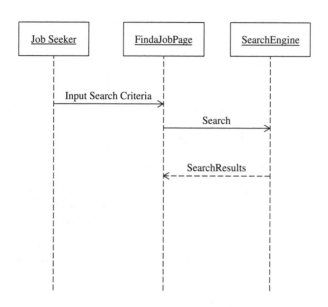

Figure 4-9 A poor design for searching for listed jobs.

validate it or not. We know nothing about the search engine—what it does or where it retrieves the data from—and we haven't any clue about the form of the results. This sequence would need several notes and a lot of verbal support. We can do better (Figure 4-10).

In the revised search sequence, we are showing that we are using a parameter object—"SearchCriteria"—to store, validate, and pass the user-entered search information. We are also depicting that the search engine reads the job listings from a database object—at this point the database object simply might represent a data access layer—and the database object puts the read information into a typed collection of "JobListing" objects. The new sequence is something we can actually implement with very little ambiguity.

Another implicit feature of the new sequence in Figure 4-10 is that others will now clearly understand that we intend to use custom objects for "JobListing." Before proceeding with implementation, we could have a discussion about the design. In addition, because the pieces are more clearly delineated, we could divide the work among specialists across the implementation team.

NOTE *The role specialization is at least as old as Adam Smith's* Wealth of Nations *or Henry Ford's assembly lines but is really just catching on in the software industry. Our relatively young industry still seems to prefer generalists and suffers as a result.*

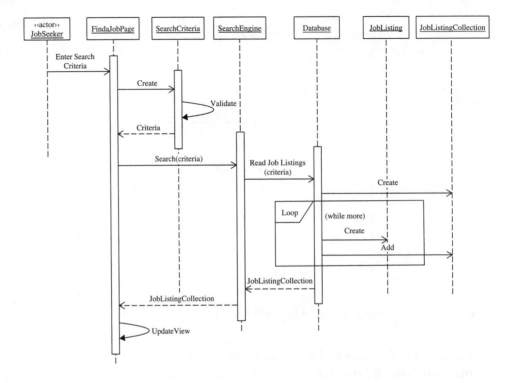

Figure 4-10   The Motown-jobs.com search behavior with a detailed sequence diagram.

Elements of Collaboration (or Communication) Diagrams

A *collaboration diagram*—redubbed a *communication diagram* in UML version 2.0—conveys the same information as a sequence diagram. Where time ordering is implicit in the linear layout of a sequence diagram, we explicitly indicate the time ordering by numbering the messages in geometrically organized collaboration diagrams.

Key symbols in collaboration diagrams are the rectangle, called a *classifier role*, and a line indicating the message, again called a *connector*. The classifier role represents the objects. Connectors represent connected objects, and a named arrow indicates the message as well as the sender and receiver. Figure 4-11 shows the sequence in Figure 4-10 converted to a collaboration diagram.

As you can see, the collaboration has the same elements but fewer details. The compact nature and fewer elements make collaborations convenient when doodling

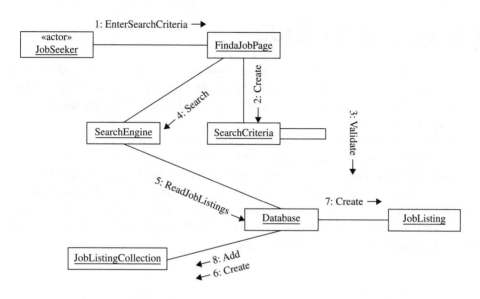

Figure 4-11 Searching for job listings represented in a collaboration diagram.

designs. To read the diagram, start with message 1 and follow the messages by number. Collaborations aren't meant to use interaction frames and, as a result, don't convey as much information as the sequence diagram.

Note the numbering scheme in Figure 4-11. I have always used a simple numbering scheme such as the one depicted in this figure, but valid UML version 2.0 requires a nested numbering scheme. A simple number scheme is 1, 2, 3, 4, etc. The UML version 2.0 nested number scheme is 1.1, 1.2, 2.1, 2.2, etc. The nested numbering scheme is designed to show nested message calls, but it can get out of hand quickly. If you want to use the UML version 2.0 numbering scheme, then the messages would be renumbered as follows: 1 remains 1, 2 becomes 1.1, 3 becomes 1.1.1, 4 becomes 1.2, 5 becomes 2, 6 becomes 2.1, 7 becomes 2.2, and 8 becomes 2.3.

TIP Consider using collaboration diagrams when working on a whiteboard or napkins—or wherever you doodle your inspired designs. The compact nature and fewer adornments of collaboration diagrams make them more manageable when designing manually.

Collaboration diagrams have other common elements such as notes, constraints, and stereotypes. These elements are used the same way they are used in sequence diagrams.

Equating Design to Code

Interaction diagrams provide you with enough information to begin coding. The objects are instances of classes, so you need to define a class for each object. Messages generally equate to methods, and the method is placed in the class of the receiver (not the caller).

I have found generally that with sequences I have most of the information I need to start writing code. How the code is implemented is based on a couple of factors: (1) your experience and (2) the implementation language. For example, "JobListing" and "JobListingCollection" represent a class and a collection containing objects of that class. If we were to implement this in C#, then "JobListingCollection" could inherit from "System.Collections.CollectionBase," and that decision drives its implementation (see the listing).

```csharp
public class JobListing
{}

public class JobListingCollection: System.Collections.CollectionBase
{
        public JobListing this[int index]
        {
                get{return (JobListing)List[index];}
                set{List[index] = value;}
        }

        public int Add(JobListing value)
        {
                return List.Add(value);
        }
}
```

Notice that in this listing I inherit from a specific base collection and define a property called *this* and the add method shown in the sequence. It is important to note that the designed sequence didn't indicate the *this* property or the parent class; sequence diagrams won't. In this instance the implementation language—Microsoft C# and the .NET framework—drove this part of the decision. Also notice that the job listing doesn't tell us anything; its an empty class. Well, the "JobListing" in the sequence didn't tell us anything either. Sequence diagrams aren't good at specifying code details. We did, however, stub out interfaces. At this point it depends on the experience of your developers how much code they can write. Less experienced developers will need more details, and more experienced developers will need fewer details. I tend to model detail that is sufficient for my audience—the developers doing the implementation.

To begin to specify more details, such as properties, supporting methods, and inheritance relationships, we can use class diagrams. Chapter 5 goes into greater depth about class diagrams.

Keep in mind that there is a lot of implicit knowledge at this stage. First, you should know that your design is likely to change. Second, things such as typed collections are based on patterns, and as is demonstrated in the code listing, implementation is driven by the language and framework. Third, there are many common and popular design patterns (see Erich Gamma et al., *Design Patterns.* Reading, MA: Addison Wesley, 1995), and it isn't always necessary to do much more than state that a pattern is used; you aren't absolutely required to create models for well-known public patterns. And last but not least, there is a subject known as *refactoring*. Refactoring is a methodical means of simplifying code. Refactoring stems from a doctoral thesis by William Opdike and a well-publicized book by Martin Fowler (see *Refactoring: Improving the Design of Existing Code.* Reading, MA: Addison Wesley, 1999). When refactoring is employed, it may mean in practice that a design decision can be improved on during implementation. If the refactoring is better than the design, then go ahead and modify the code and simply update the model to reflect the change.

NOTE   *We demonstrated a refactoring in design in Figures 4-9 and 4-10 when we introduced the "SearchCriteria" object. This refactoring is named "Introduce Parameter Object," which simply replaces a long list of parameters with a single instance of a parameter class that contains those values. We also snuck in a design pattern, "Iterator." The strongly typed collection implemented as a response to Figure 4-10's typed collection of "JobListing" objects inherits from .NET's CollectionBase, which, in turn, implements an IEnumerable pattern (an implementation of the iterator pattern). Good designs and implementations are based on patterns and refactorings. Good design models are based on a simple, accurate, and direct use of the UML and incorporate design patterns and refactorings.*

Quiz

1. A sequence diagram is an example of
    a. a collaboration diagram.
    b. an interaction diagram.
    c. a class diagram.
    d. a use case diagram.

2. Sequence diagrams depict all the objects that support a single use case.

   a. True

   b. False

3. Sequence diagrams are good at showing how to implement lines of code.

   a. True

   b. False

4. A collaboration diagram and a communication diagram differ

   a. because collaboration diagrams show that objects interact and communication diagrams show how objects communicate.

   b. not at all; collaboration diagrams simply were renamed in UML version 2.0.

   c. because collaboration diagrams are geometric and communication diagrams are linear.

   d. Both a and c

5. Sequence diagrams can model asynchronous and multithreaded behavior.

   a. True

   b. False

6. Interaction frames use a guard condition to control when and which fragment of the frame to execute.

   a. True

   b. False

7. The alt—called an *interaction operator*—interaction frame

   a. is used to show an invalid fragment.

   b. models optional behavior.

   c. shows conditional logic.

   d. models parallel behavior.

8. A good design must include both sequence and collaboration diagrams.

   a. True

   b. False

9. Activation symbols are used to show

   a. the lifetime of an object in a sequence diagram.

   b. the lifetime of an object in a communication diagram.

c. when an object is created.

d. None of the above

10. Valid UML version 2.0 employs

   a. a nested numbering scheme to show time ordering in a sequence diagram.

   b. a nested number scheme to show time ordering in a communication diagram.

   c. a simple numbering scheme to show time ordering in a sequence diagram.

   d. a simple numbering scheme to show time ordering in a collaboration diagram.

Answers

1. b

2. a

3. b

4. b

5. a

6. a

7. c

8. b

9. a

10. b

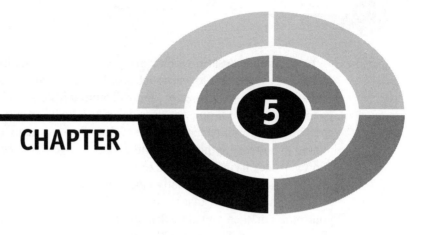

CHAPTER

5

What Are the Things That Describe My Problem?

This chapter introduces *class diagrams.* Class diagrams are the most common and the most important view of the design that you will create. Class diagrams are called *static diagrams* because they don't depict action. What class diagrams do is show you things and their relationships. Class diagrams are designed to show all the pieces of your solution—which pieces are related to or used as parts of new wholes—and should convey a sense of the system to be built at rest.

To communicate at a technically precise level in Unified Modeling Language (UML)–speak, it helps to learn such words as *association, composition, aggregation, generalization*, and *realization*, but to communicate sufficiently and effectively, all you must know are simple words to describe whole and part relationships, i.e., parent and child relationships, and be able to describe how many of a thing of one sort are related to how many things of another sort. I will introduce the technical terms, but don't get stuck trying to memorize them. With practice, eventually you will incorporate UML-speak into your daily language.

A common myth is that if you find all the nouns and all the verbs that describe your problem, then you have discovered all the classes and methods you will need. This is incorrect. The truth is that the nouns and verbs that describe your problem sufficiently for a user are the easiest classes to find and can help you to complete a useful analysis of the problem, but you will end up designing and using many more classes that are necessary to fill in the blanks.

This chapter will show you how to create class diagrams and begin helping you to figure out how to find most or all of the classes you will need to design a solution. An important concept here is that very few designs require that all details be discovered before programming ensues. (A few agencies and companies, such as NASA and General Dynamics, may have rigid requirements that stipulate the completeness of a design, but in most instances this leads to very long production times and excessive expense.)

In this chapter I will show you how to use the elements of class diagrams, create class diagrams, and capture some advance ideas, and I will show you some ways to discover some less obvious classes and behaviors. You will learn how to

- Identify and use class diagram elements
- Create simple but useful class diagrams
- Model some advanced expressions
- Figure out how to discover less obvious supporting classes and behaviors

Elements of Basic Class Diagrams

Foolishly, in high school I didn't like literature class and was stupefied by grammar classes. Fortunately, by college, I began to see the error of my thinking. While I am not an expert on English grammar, understanding such things as prepositions, prepositional phrases, conjunctions, objects, subjects, verbs, verb tense, adjectives, adverbs, articles, active voice and passive voice, and plural and singular possessive words helps a lot when writing these passages. The reason I tell you this is that, unfortunately, grammar is a component of the UML because it is a language, but the UML's grammar is much easier than English grammar. How much easier is the UML? The answer is that the two most important elements in class diagrams, as in other diagrams, is a rectangle and a line. The rectangles are classes, and the lines are connectors showing the relationship between those classes.

UML class diagrams can seem as challenging as Shakespeare's *Hamlet* or as easy as the prose in Hemingway's *The Sun Also Rises*, but both can tell a story equally well. As a general rule, focus on the classes and their relationships, and use more advanced elements, which I also will discuss, when needed. Avoid the idea that a class diagram has to be decorated extensively to be useful.

Understanding Classes and Objects

The rectangle in a class diagram is called a *classifier*. The classifier can tell you the name of the class and the name of an instance of that class, called an *object*. Classes ultimately will include behaviors and attributes, collectively called *features*, too. Attributes can be fields, properties, or both. Behaviors will be realized as methods (Figure 5-1).

Significantly, class diagrams will use the simple classifier represented by the "Motorcycle" class in Figure 5-1. The other types are important and worth exploring. Let's take a moment to do that.

TIP   When you first start capturing classes in your models, conceptually thought of as an analysis phase, it is sufficient to start with just classes and relationships. Features can be added later.

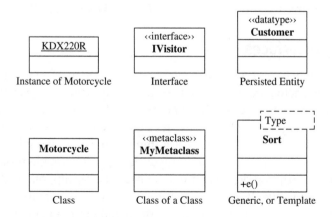

Figure 5-1   Examples of classifiers in the UML.

Using Simple Classes

The class (shown in Figure 5-1 as "Motorcycle") is the most common element in a class diagram. Classes ultimately are things in your analysis and design and may be domain-specific things or supporting things. Consider the example given in the next two paragraphs.

Groves Motorsports in Mason, Michigan, sells motorcycles, ATVs, snowmobiles, and accessories. If we were designing an inventory system for Groves Motorsports, then salespeople, purchasers, and mechanics could tell us about motorcycles, ATVs, snowmobiles, boots, helmets, and related sales items. From this discussion we might easily derive starter classes such as "SalesItem" and "Motorcycle." Suppose now that we have to manage the inventory using a relational database. Now we need to know what kind of database and what the classes are that describe how we interact with inventory items, i.e., how we read and write the inventory.

The result is that one class diagram may have classes that describe inventory items, but other class diagrams may describe elements such as promotions and sales, financing, and managing items that are not for sale but may be part of the inventory of items in for maintenance. The hard part of design is finding and describing these relationships. A motorcycle is still a motorcycle whether it is for sale or in for service, and we can use the same "Motorcycle" class, but we will need to show different kinds of relationships based on a particular instance of that class.

Using Objects

A kind of a class diagram is an *object diagram*. Object diagrams show instances of classes and their relationships. In the UML, an object is distinguished from a class by underlining the name in the top compartment of the rectangle. This is illustrated in Figure 5-1 by my midlife-crisis-inspired Kawasaki KDX 220R.

Using Interfaces

Programmers often have trouble with interfaces (see "IVisitor" in Figure 5-1). *Interfaces* are equivalent to pure abstract classes. By saying an interface is purely abstract, I am saying that an interface will have no executable code. Interfaces are a critical element in class diagrams and software; let's take a moment to understand why.

When I use *inheritance*, I mean that a thing also can be thought of as another kind of thing. For example, both a motorcycle and an ATV are kinds of recreational vehicles. This description depicts an inheritance relationship, one that doesn't use an interface. Comparatively, a remote control sends infrared signals to change channel, attenuate volume, begin recording, or open and close a garage door. Devices that receive these signals may not be related. For instance, a TV and a garage door opener both have an up and down feature, and garage door openers and televisions are sold with remote controls, but a garage door opener is not a kind of television or vice versa, but each may have the ability to perform an up and down operation. Up and down increase or decrease the volume of a television, or up and down raise and lower a garage door. This ability that supports up and down through a remote device is an *interface* or a *related facet* of each of the unrelated devices. How this behavior is implemented is also completely unrelated but doesn't have to be.

Interfaces are used when parts of things have semantically similar facets—up and down behaviors—but have no related genealogy.

By convention we use the interface stereotype and prefix interfaces with "I," as shown in Figure 5-1. Considering the "IVisitor" interface in Figure 5-1, we could say that visitors have a *kind* feature. Fleas can visit a dog, and your brother-in-law can visit your house, but a flea is a kind of dog visitor and your brother-in-law Amos is a kind of family visitor. Fleas and Amos are not similar kinds of things (no parasitic pun similarities intended).

Using Datatypes

The «datatype» stereotype usually is used to show simple datatypes such as "Integer." If you were designing a programming language, then your class diagrams might show datatypes, but in general, I model these elements as attributes of classes and reserve classifiers for compound types such as "Motorcycle" and "JobListing."

Using Parameterized or Generic Types

Synonyms can make life confusing. In the UML, *parameterized types* mean the same thing as *generics* in C# and Java and *templates* in C++. A parameterized class is a class whose primary data type is specified at runtime. To understand parameterized classes, consider a classic example.

What does a sort algorithm sort? The answer is that a sort algorithm can sort anything. Numbers, names, inventory, income tax brackets, or job listings all can be sorted. By separating the datatype—number, string, "JobListing"—from the algorithm, you have a parameterized type. Parameterized classes are used to separate implementation from datatype. The "Sort" class in Figure 5-1 shows that a parameterized type uses the rectangle with a dashed smaller rectangle specifying the parameter type.

It is worth noting that using templates well is considered an advanced part of software design and that a tremendous amount of great software exists without templates.

Using Metaclasses

A *metaclass* is a class of a class. This seems to have evolved to address the problem of obtaining runtime type information about classes. In practice, a metaclass can be passed around like an object. Metaclasses are supported directly in languages such as Delphi; e.g., given a class "JobListing," we could define a metaclass and (by convention) name it "TJobListing," passing instances of "TJobListing" as a parameter. The metaclass "TJobListing" could be used to create instances of "JobListing." In a language such as C#, metaclasses are not supported directly. Instead, C# uses a "Type" object that represents sort of an instance of a universal metaclass; i.e., every class has an associated metaobject that knows everything about classes of that type. Again, in C#, the "Type" class exists to support dynamic, runtime discovery about classes.

NOTE *There is another concept,* metadata, *that is similar to the notion of metaclasses. However, metadata are data that describe data and often are used to convey additional information about data; e.g., metadata sometimes are used to describe valid values for data. Suppose that you were writing an accounting system and that valid invoice dates were January 1, 1990, to time's end. Most datetypes support dates much earlier than 1/1/1990, but you could use a date metadata object to indicate that for your purposes valid dates began on 1/1/1990 instead of the earliest date for your language's datetype.*

There are some practical applications for metaclasses. In Delphi, metaclasses are used to support creating a control that is dragged from the control panel (toolbox) to a form at design time. In .NET, the "Type" object—a kind of implementation of the metaclass—is used to support dynamically loading, creating, and using objects. Microsoft calls this capability "Reflection," but it is basically an implementation of the metaclass idiom. Consequently, when the Delphi or Visual Studio designers were designing their respective tools, they may have used the metaclass classifier in their UML models, assuming that they used UML models. It is important to recognize that just as different UML tools will support differing levels of UML compatibility, different languages will support various design decisions in different ways.

Decorating Classes

The classifier symbol is divided into rectangular regions (see the "Motorcycle" class in Figure 5-1). The top-most rectangle contains the name of the class and the class stereotypes. The second rectangular region from the top contains attributes (Figure 5-2). As shown in Figure 5-2, the "Motorcycle" class has an attribute "motor." The bottom rectangle contains behaviors (or methods). In Figure 5-2, the "Motorcyle" class contains a method named "GetPowerOutput."

Each of the attributes and methods can be decorated with access modifiers. (Remember that the term *feature* generically means "method or attribute.") The

Motorcycle
–motor
+GetPowerOutput()

Figure 5-2   The "Motorcycle" class with a private access modifier on a motor attribute.

features can be decorated with the access modifiers +, –, or #. The plus (+) symbol means that a feature is public, or available for external consumption. The minus (–) symbol means that a feature is private, or for internal consumption, and the pound (#) symbol means that a feature is neither public nor private. Usually, the pound symbol means that a feature is for internal consumption or consumption by child classes. The pound symbol usually equates to a protected member. Generally, UML tools will make methods public by default and attributes private by default.

Using Attributes

Many modern languages distinguish between properties and fields. A *field* represents what your classes know, and a *property* represents an implicit function for reading and writing to private fields. It is not necessary to capture both fields and properties; capturing fields is enough.

When you add classes to your class diagrams, add the fields, and make them private. It is up to those implementing your designs to add property methods if they are supported. If your language does not support properties, then during implementation, use methods such as get_*Field1* and set_*Field1* for each field to constrain access to a class's data.

Tip   *Adding private fields and relying on an implicit understanding that fields are accessed through methods, whether public or private, is a good recommended practice but not enforced or part of the UML. This style of design implementation simply is considered a best practice.*

Declaring Attributes

Attributes are shown as a line of text. They need an access modifier to determine visibility. Attributes need to include a name, can include a datatype and default value, and can have other modifiers that indicate if the attribute is read only, write only, static, or something else.

In Figure 5-2, the "motor" attribute has a private access modifier and a name only. Here are some more complete attribute declarations containing examples of the elements we discussed:

–Type : MotorType = MotorType.TwoStroke
–Size : string = "220cc"
–Brand : string = "Kawasaki" {read-only}

In this listing we have a private attribute named "Type," whose datatype is "Motor-Type," and its default value is "MotorType.TwoStroke." We have an attribute named "Size" with a datatype of "string" and a default value of "220cc." And the last attribute is a string named "Brand" with a default value of "Kawasaki"; the "Brand" attribute is read only.

Declaring Attributes with Association

Attributes also can be depicted as an *association*. This just means that the attribute is modeled as a class with a connector between the containing class and the class of the attribute. All the elements mentioned previously can be present; they simply are arranged differently.

Consider the "motor" attribute shown in Figure 5-2. This attribute could refer to an association to a "Motor" class (Figure 5-3); further, the attributes—"Type," "Size," and "Brand"—could be listed as members of the "Motor" class.

When you use an association attribute, leave the field declaration out of the class. The association link (shown as "motor") in Figure 5-3 plays that role; there is no need to repeat the declaration directly in the containing class. The association connector is named. This name represents the name of the field; in Figure 5-3 the name is "motor," and the class is "Motor." Association attributes also can include a *multiplicity*, which indicates how many of each item is involved in the association. In the example, one motorcycle has one motor. If the relationship were "Airplanes" and "Motors," then we might have an asterisk next to the "Motor" class to indicate that planes can have more than one motor.

TIP *Some conventions use an article prefix for an association name, such as "the" or "a," as in "theMotor" or "aMotor."*

The class diagram in Figure 5-3 conveys identical information to the class diagram in Figure 5-4. Class diagrams can quickly become overly complex if all the

Figure 5-3   Showing the "motor" attribute using an association.

Motorcycle
–motor : Motor

Figure 5-4   This figure conveys information identical to that shown in Figure 5-4; i.e., a motorcycle contains a motor whose type is "Motor."

attributes are modeled as associations. A good rule of thumb is to show simple types as field declarations in the containing class and show compound types (classes) as association attributes. Figure 5-5 shows how we can elaborate on the "Motor" class more completely by using an association attribute rather than just a "motor" field. (Figure 5-5 adds the fields used to describe a motor mentioned earlier.)

In Figure 5-5, we mean that only one motorcycle has a 220-cc two-stroke Kawasaki motor. (This is probably not true in real life, but that's what the model conveys.)

NOTE   *I mentioned that the diagram in Figure 5-5 means that only one motorcycle has a 220-cc two-stroke Kawasaki motor, but that this information may be inaccurate. By doing so, I inadvertently reillustrated one of the values of class diagrams: A class diagram is a picture that means something, and experts can look at it and quickly tell you if you have captured something that is factual and useful.*

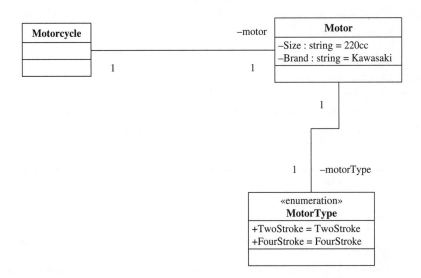

Figure 5-5   This class diagram contains more information about the motorcycle's motor by using an association attribute for the motor and a second association attribute for the possible types of motors.

Attribute Arrays and Multiplicity

A single attribute type might represent more than one of that type. This implies multiplicity and possibly attribute ordering. There can be more than one of something; e.g., multiengined planes might be modeled as a plane with an array of engines, and arrays can be sorted or unsorted. Multiplicity is indicated most readily by adding a count to an association attribute, and sorted or unsorted attributes can be annotated using the words *ordered* or *unordered* in brackets. Table 5-1 shows the possible multiplicity counts and provides a description for each.

Multiplicity indicators are used in other contexts and have the same count meaning when applied to other UML elements beside attribute associations.

Tip *If the upper and lower values are identical, then use a single-valued multiplicity indicator such as 1 instead of 1..1.*

When speaking about multiplicities, you might hear the terms *optional* applied to multiplicities with a lower bound of 1, *mandatory* if at least one is required, *single-valued* if only one is permitted, and *multivalued* if an asterisk is used.

Indicating Uniqueness

Attributes can be annotated to indicate uniqueness. For example, if a field represents a key in a hashtable or primary key in a relational database, then it may be useful to annotate that attribute with the {unique} or {nonunique} modifiers. For instance, if you want to indicate that "JobListingID" is a uniquely valued field, then define it in the class as follows:

–JobListingID : integer {unique}

If you want to indicate that the key value of a collection must be unique, then use the {unique} modifier. If keys can be repeated, then use {nonunique}. Rarely do modelers have so much time that they use very detailed diagrams that include {nonordered} and {unique} to mean hashtable. Generally, modelers simply express the datatype

1	Only 1
*	Many
0..1	Zero or 1
0..*	A lower bound of zero and an upper bound of infinity; this is equivalent to *
1..1	One and only one; this is equivalent to 1
1..*	A lower bound of at least one and an upper bound of infinity
m,n	Meaning a noncontiguous multiplicity such as 3 or 5; no longer valid UML

Table 5-1   Mutiplicity Indicators

of the attribute, but it is worth knowing that the UML specifies ordered versus non-ordered and unique versus nonunique and not array or hashtable. Arrays and hashtables represent known design solutions, not aspects of the UML language.

Adding Operations to Classes

It can be useful to think of modeling as something that cycles from a high-level macro view to successively lower-level micro views and ultimately to code, the most detailed micro view. The macro phase can be thought of as an analysis phase. During this phase, it might be enough to capture classes and relationships as you begin to understand the problem space. As your understanding improves and you begin to capture the details of a solution—moving from a macro understanding to a more detailed micro understanding—you begin elaborating on a design. At this juncture you may return to your class diagrams and begin adding operations and attributes. Operations, behaviors, and methods all refer to the same thing. In the UML, we generally say *operation*, and when coding, we generally say *method.*

Operations are shown in the bottom-most rectangle of a classifier. Operations have a visibility modifier such as attributes. Operations include a return datatype; a name; a parameter list including names, datatypes, and modifiers; and additional modifiers that may indicate if an operation is static, virtual, or something else.

As mentioned previously, it isn't necessary to show property methods. You also can save yourself some time by not elaborating on nonpublic operations in great detail. The public operations generally will describe the behaviors of the class sufficiently, and the nonpublic members can be left to the devices of your programmers.

Since I don't actually have an application that represents motorcycles or a vehicle inventory for a motor sports vehicle store, let's change the examples a bit. Occasionally, I go to Las Vegas and partake in a little "BlackJack" (Figure 5-6). Because I like to get as much entertainment as possible for my money, I wanted to practice "BlackJack" in a way that would make me a better player. Hence I wrote a "BlackJack" game that provided tips based on the best course of action to win a hand. (This application is done, and the code is online at *www.softconcepts.com.*) In that example, there are many classes, including a class that represents a player's hand as a list of cards. Some of the operation signatures used to implement the "Hand" class are shown in the classifier in Figure 5-7.

Modeling Relationships in Class Diagrams

Class diagrams consist primarily of classifiers with attributes and operations and connectors that describe the relationships between classes. About 80 percent of your class diagrams will just use these features. However, while this sounds simple, class

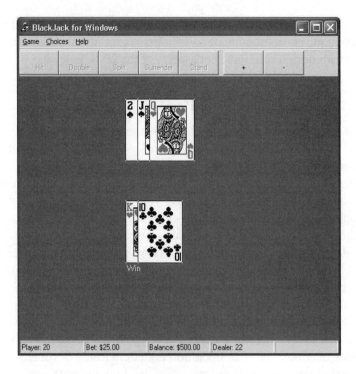

Figure 5-6   The "BlackJack for Windows" game.

diagrams can be used to describe some very advanced relationships. By name, these relationships include generalization, inheritance, realization, composition, aggregation, dependency, and association. Refined further, the connectors that depict these

Hand
+Add(in card : Card) : int
+New() : void
+GetTextHand() : string
+TextPrintHand() : void
+IsBlackJack() : bool
+IsBust() : bool
+BustedAtValue() : int
+GetHandValueLow() : int
+GetHandValueHigh() : int
+GetBestValue() : int
#GetHandWidth() : int
+GraphicPrintHand(in g : Graphics, in x : int, in y : int, in cardWidth : int, in cardHeight : int, in focused : bool) : void
+Stand() : void
+Dump() : void

Figure 5-7   A classifier showing several of the operation signatures for the "Hand" class.

relationships can be directed or undirected and bidirectional or unidirectional and can express multiplicity (just like attribute multiplicity). In this section I will introduce these connectors, but I will wait until Chapter 6 to explore examples in more detail.

Modeling Associations

The association connector is a solid line. If it is directed, then the solid line can have a stick-figure arrow at either or both ends. For example, in the preceding section I implied that a blackjack "Hand" was comprised of "Card" objects. I could model this relationship by adding a "Card" class to the "Hand" class introduced in Figure 5-7 and connecting the "Hand" and "Card" classifiers with an association connector. Look at Figure 5-5 for a visual example of two associations, one between "Motorcycle" and "Motor" and another between "Motor" and "MotorType."

Just as in Figure 5-5, associations can specify multiplicity at either end of the connector. Figure 5-5 indicates that a "Motorcycle" is associated with one "Motor," and Figure 5-8 indicates that there is at least one hand and that each hand can contain many cards.

If there is an arrow at either end of an association (Figure 5-8), then the association is said to be *directed* or *directional*. The end with the arrow is the target or the object that can be navigated to. The end without the arrow is called the *source*. *Navigation* simply means that the source—"Hand" in Figure 5-8—has an attribute of the target's type—"Card." If the association were bidirectional, then "Hand" would have a "Card" attribute, and "Card" would have a "Hand" attribute. If the association were nondirected—there are no arrows—then a bidirectional association is assumed.

Modeling Aggregation and Composition

Aggregation and composition have to do with whole and part relationships. The connector for aggregation is a hollow diamond, a straight line, and optionally a stick-figure arrow. The diamond is attached to the whole classifier, and the arrow is attached to the part classifier. A composition connector looks like an aggregation connector except that the diamond is filled in.

Figure 5-8   "Hand" and "Card" are associated unidirectionally, which means that "Hand" has an attribute "Card."

Figuring out how to use aggregation and composition can be decided very simply. Aggregation is syntactical sugar and is no different from an association—you don't need it. Composition is aggregation, except that the whole class is responsible for creating and destroying the part class, and the part class cannot exist in any other relationship at the same time. For example, a motorcycle's engine cannot be in a second motorcycle at the same time—that's composition. As Fowler says, there is a "no sharing" rule in a composition relationship, but part objects can be shared in association and aggregation relationships.

Before you look at Figure 5-9, compare aggregation (or association) with composition by thinking of the popular poker game Texas hold 'em. In Texas hold 'em, every player gets two cards, and then five cards are dealt. Every player makes the best five-card hand possible by using his or her two cards and the five shared cards. That is, every player's hand is an aggregate of five of the seven cards, five of which are available to all players; i.e., five cards are shared. If we were writing a software version of Texas hold 'em using our "Hand" abstraction, then every player would have a reference to the five shared cards. Figure 5-9 shows aggregation on the left and composition on the right.

Modeling Inheritance

It is important to keep in mind that the UML is a distinct language, distinct from your favorite object-oriented programming language and distinct from object-oriented programming languages in general. Thus, to be a UML modeler, one has to be multilingual; UML modelers need to speak UML, and it really helps to speak the object-oriented language that will be used to implement the design. In UML-speak, inheritance is *generalization*. This means that programmers may say *inheritance* when they mean *generalization*, and when they say *generalization*, they may mean *inheritance*.

NOTE *Unfortunately, inheritance relationships suffer from a plethora of synonyms. Inheritance, generalization, and is-a all refer to the same thing. The words* parent *and* child *are also referred to as* superclass *or* base class *and* subclass. *Base, parent, and* superclass *all mean the same thing.* Child *and* subclass *mean the same thing. The terms you hear depend on whom you are talking to. To make matters worse, sometimes these words are used incorrectly.*

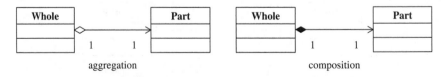

Figure 5-9 Aggregation is semantically identical to association, and composition means that the composite class is the only class that has a reference to the owned class.

Generalization refers to an *is-a* or substitutability relationship and is reflected in a UML class diagram by a solid line connector with a hollow triangle at one end. The triangle points at the parent, and the other end is connected to the child.

In an *inheritance relationship*, the child class gets all the features of the parent and then can add some features of its own. Polymorphism works because child classes are substitutable for parent classes. *Substitutability* means that if an operation or statement is defined to use an argument of a parent type, then any child type can be substituted for the parent. Consider the Motown-jobs.com (*www.motown-jobs. com*) example. If a class "Listing" is defined as a parent class and "Résumé," "Job," and "Advertisement" are defined as child classes to the parent "Listing," then anywhere a "Listing" argument is defined, it can be substituted with one of "Résumé," "Job," or "Advertisement." This relationship is shown in Figure 5-10.

Any public or protected member of "Listing" becomes a member of "Job," "Résumé," and "Advertisement." Private members are implicitly part of "Job," "Résumé," and "Advertisement," but these child classes—and any child classes— cannot access private members of the parent class (or parent classes if multiple inheritance is supported).

Modeling Realizations

Realization relationships refer to inheriting from or realizing interfaces. The connector is almost identical to a generalization connector except that the connector line is a dashed line with a hollow triangle instead of a solid line with a hollow triangle. When a class realizes, or inherits from, an interface, the class is basically agreeing that it will provide an implementation for the features declared by the interface. Figure 5-11 shows the visual representation of a "Radio" class realizing the

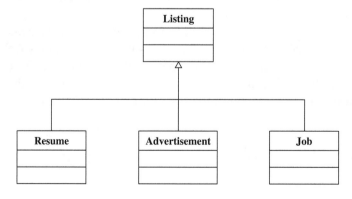

Figure 5-10   This figure shows that "Résumé," "Job," and "Advertisement" all inherit from "Listing."

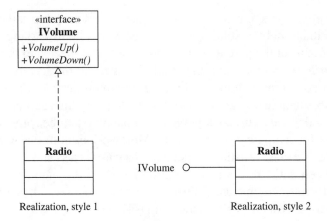

Realization, style 1   Realization, style 2

Figure 5-11   Realization, or interface inheritance, can be shown in either style, as depicted in the figure.

"IVolume" interface. (Keep in mind that the "I" prefix is simply a convention and not part of the UML.)

To help you become familiar with interface inheritance, I added an alternate style on the right of Figure 5-11. Many modeling tools support both styles. Pick one style, and stick with it. (I prefer the style on the left in Figure 5-11, which is the style described in the preceding paragraph.)

Modeling Dependency

The *dependency relationship* is one of client and supplier. One class, the *client*, is dependent on a second class, the *supplier*, to provide a service. The symbol for a dependency relationship looks like a unidirectional association except that the line is dashed instead of solid (Figure 5-12).

Suppose, for example, that we decide to support several presentation styles to users of "BlackJack." We might offer a console, Windows, or a Web graphical user interface (GUI). Next, we could define a method "Print" that is dependent on a specific "CardPrinter." If the "CardPrinter" is a graphical printer, then we might display a bitmap of the card, but if the "CardPrinter" is a DOS-based printer, then

Figure 5-12   In this figure we are conveying that the "Card" is dependent on the "CardPrinter," where "Card" is the client and "CardPrinter" is the supplier.

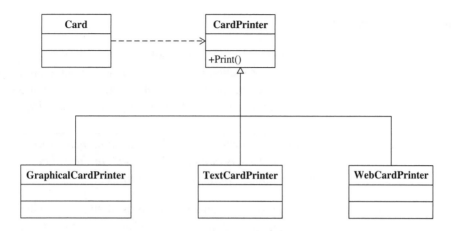

Figure 5-13   The dependency relationship now includes generalization showing specific kinds of "CardPrinter" objects.

maybe we just write text to the console. Figure 5-13 shows the dependency relationship combined with generalization to reflect a variety of "CardPrinter" classes.

TIP   *It is worth noting that Figure 5-13 introduces a concept: It is a good practice to capture various facets of a design in separate diagrams. For example, in Figure 5-13, we may not be showing all the classes in the game "BlackJack," but we are showing useful relationships between the "Card" class and classes that supply printing.*

Another useful feature is that connectors such as dependency are associated with predefined stereotypes. A stereotype adds meaning. We will explore stereotypes in Chapter 6 when we explore how classes are related in greater detail.

Stereotyping Classes

The *stereotype* is a means by which the UML can be extended and evolve. Visually, stereotypes appear between guillemots («stereotype»). There are several predefined stereotypes for UML symbols such as the classifier, and you are free to adopt new stereotypes if the need arises. Figure 5-11 shows an example where the «interface» stereotype was used to indicate that a classifier represents an interface.

TIP   *Some UML modeling tools will replace stereotypes with specific symbols, changing the way a diagram looks, although the meaning is unchanged. For example, both the classifier with the «interface» stereotype and the hollow circle in Figure 5-11 accurately reflect the interface "IVolume."*

Using Packages

The *package* symbol looks like a file folder. This symbol (Figure 5-14) is used generically to represent a higher level of abstraction than the classifier. Although a package commonly may be implemented as a namespace or subsystem, with a stereotype, a package can be used for general organization and simply represent a file folder.

Tip *Namespaces solved a long-time problem of multiple development teams using identical names for classes. A class named "Customer" in the Softconcepts namespace is distinct from "Customer" in the IBM namespace.*

The game "BlackJack" uses the APIs contained in the cards.dll that ships with Windows (and is used in games such as Solitaire). We could use two packages and a dependency to show that the game "BlackJack" is dependent on the APIs in cards.dll.

Using Notes and Comments

Annotating diagrams is an important aspect of modeling. The note is supported in class diagrams, but see if you can convey as much meaning as possible without adding a lot of notes. (See Figure 5-15 for an example of the dog-eared note symbol used in the UML.)

Many tools support model documentation that is stored with the model but not displayed in the diagrams. Specific model documentation beyond notes, comments, and constraints is not an actual part of the UML but is a good adjunct to creating models.

Constraints

Constraints use the same dog-eared symbol in every diagram. Constraints actually can be a deceptively complex part of the UML and can include information that greatly helps code generators. For instance, constraints can be written in plain text or in Object Constraint Language (OCL). While I will provide examples of constraints throughout this book, a discussion of OCL is intentionally omitted as not very demystifying.

Figure 5-14   The diagram shows that the "BlackJack" package is dependent on the package "cards.dll," which uses the «subsystem» stereotype.

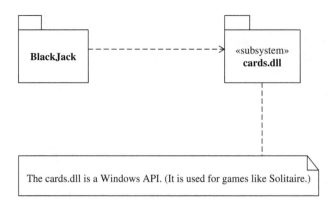

Figure 5-15 The dog-eared rectangle is used to attach notes or comments to elements of UML diagrams.

To demonstrate a constraint, we can add the constraint symbol and enter a text constraint that states that the number of cards in a "Deck" must be 52 (Figure 5-16). It is also possible to express this without a constraint by changing the end multiplicity from * to the number 52. Another example might be a constraint that expresses

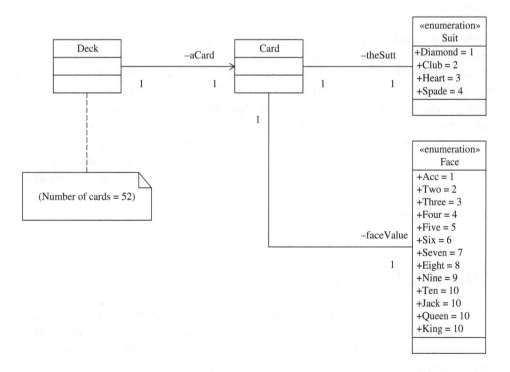

Figure 5-16 This figure illustrates how we can mix in constraints—"Number of cards = 52" in the figure—with other diagram elements to add precision to a diagram.

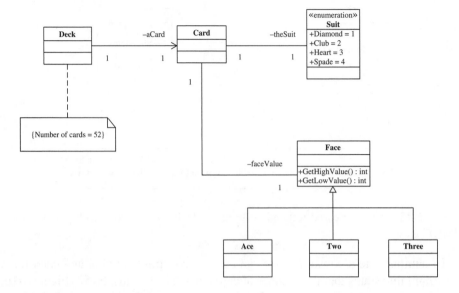

Figure 5-17   The class diagram from Figure 5-16 modified to capture the fact that cards can have dynamic face values.

something about the face value or the number and variety of suits, and we also could express these elements with enumerations.

In Figure 5-16, I included the constraint that the number of cards in a "Deck" has to be 52, an enumeration to indicate that there are four suits, and an enumeration to indicate that there are 14 possible unique face values. Unfortunately, the figure still falls short because in the game "BlackJack," the ace does not have a unique, single value. An analysis of this model with a domain expert might quickly reveal a possible problem with using an enumeration for "Face." Because of the dual value of the ace, we may elect to redesign the solution to use a class—"Face"—and a generalization—specific face values, such as "Ace," "Two," "Three," etc.—to fix the problem with aces (Figure 5-17).

Modeling Primitives

The UML defines *primitives* such as "Integer," "Boolean," "String," and "Unlimited-Natural" for use in the UML specification, but most languages and tools define their own primitive types. You can model primitives using a classifier, the «primitive» stereotype, and the name of the type.

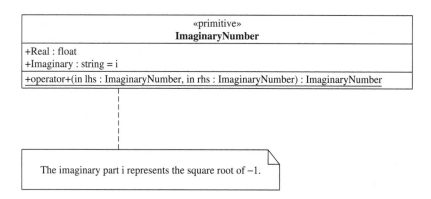

Figure 5-18   Imaginary numbers are real numbers multiplied by the imaginary number *i*, which represents the square root of –1.

Generally, primitives are modeled as attributes of other classes. However, there are instances where you may want to define your own primitives—the canonical imaginary number being an example (Figure 5-18)—and some languages such as Microsoft's Common Language Specification (CLS) for .NET where seemingly primitive types actually represent objects and are treated as such.

Sometimes it is useful to elaborate on primitives, and it is acceptable to model them as a class using the association connector, as demonstrated earlier in this chapter. The diagram in Figure 5-18 documents an "ImaginaryNumber" and elaborates on what the real and imaginary parts represent, as well as incorporating an overloaded operator—an operator function—for the primitive type.

TIP   *Languages such as C++, C#, and recently, even Visual Basic.NET support operator overloading—which means that behaviors for operators such as +, –, *, and / can be defined for new types. Modeling primitive types and languages that support operator overloading can be very useful if you need to define extended datatypes in your solution.*

Modeling Enumerations

Enumerations are named values that have a semantic meaning greater than their underlying value. For example, the integers 1, 2, 3, and 4 could be used to represent the suits in a deck of playing cards, but an enumeration type "Suit" containing four named values conveys more meaning (see Figure 5-17).

Many modern languages support a strong type system. This means that if you define an enumeration argument, then only values defined by that enumeration are

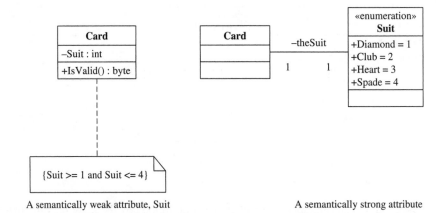

A semantically weak attribute, Suit   A semantically strong attribute

Figure 5-19   The integer "Suit" on the left needs explanation by way of a constraint to limit and clarify possible integer values, whereas the semantically stronger "Suit" enumeration on the right needs no such explanation.

suitable values, and the compiler will enforce use of the semantically more meaningful type's values. Contrasted with using a type of the underlying type—e.g., integers to represent suits—that would permit any value of the underlying type, enumerations convey more information and rigor in code and more information in UML models. This contrast is illustrated in Figure 5-19.

NOTE   *Sometimes modelers and programmers make tradeoffs. For example, we may know that a well-named enumeration may convey more meaning but elect not to use semantically stronger types anyway. Suppose that, like Lucky Charms cereal, diamonds, clubs, hearts, and spades might evolve in the future—a five-suited deck could include clovers. If we were to use an enumeration, then we'd have to open the code back up at that future time and redefine the enumeration. However, if we used an integer and stored the range of values in a database, then we could extend or change the possible values of "Suit" by executing an SQL UPDATE command. Knowing about and making these kinds of value judgments is one of those things that make software development challenging.*

Indicating Namespaces

The *namespace* is a more recent invention in OOP languages. The namespace is a way to group code elements. The problem originated as software companies began using one another's tools to a greater extent until it became more common that

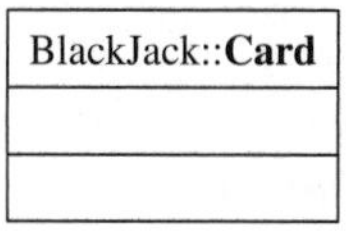

BlackJack::**Card**

Figure 5-20   Packages are often coded as namespaces and are shown in UML diagrams on the left-hand side of the scope resolution operator, a double colon.

vendor A would produce useful software with similarly named entities as vendor B. The namespace is a solution that permits two or more identically named elements to coexist in the same solution; the namespace distinguishes these elements.

Often packages are visual representations of namespaces, and namespaces can be shown in diagrams to distinguish elements with the same classifier name. The scope operator :: is used to concatenate a namespace to an element in that namespace. Namespaces can be nested, siblings, or arranged in any hierarchical way that makes sense in the context of a problem. If the "Card" class is defined as an element in the "BlackJack" namespace, then we can capture this by adding the "Card" class to the "BlackJack" package, as depicted in Figure 5-20.

Figuring Out the Classes You Need

There are two modalities for object-oriented software development: consuming and producing. Teams can work collaboratively in either or both modalities, but not understanding whether a team's skill supports consuming objects, producing objects, or both can lead to problems.

It is perfectly acceptable to use components, controls, and objects produced by others and piece together a solution as well as possible. The closest analogy to this style of development is how C++ programmers think of Visual Basic programmers (although this belief may be a bit unfair). In this modality, a team realizes that its understanding of how to use objects is good but that its own production of objects is wanting. A second acceptable modality is that a team knows that it is cognizant of design patterns, refactoring, and has a history of success in architecting object-oriented solutions, including the production of its own objects. Both modalities are acceptable, but it is important to know in which mode you have the greatest opportunity for success. (As Dirty Harry said: "A man has got to know his limitations.") If you are going to succeed at creating UML models that describe something more than classes created by experts, then you will need to know how to find classes, so let's talk about that for a few minutes.

> **NOTE** *In 2005, author Richard Mansfield, in an editorial posted on DevX.com, challenged OO as a valid paradigm. All jokes about old dogs and new tricks aside, Mansfield made a point accidentally. The point is that if you know OO well enough to consume it but try to produce it, then OO likely will be disappointing. I suspect that many OO projects fail because accomplished OO consumers are not so accomplished OO producers. Producing quality objects is difficult at best, and without extemporaneous knowledge of patterns, refactoring, and experience, good OO may be impossible to produce.*

Finding the right classes is the hardest thing you will do. Finding the right classes is much harder than drawing the diagrams. If you find the right classes, then napkins are sufficient for modeling. If you can't find the right classes, then no matter how much money you spend on tools, your designs probably will result in failed implementations.

Using the Naive Approach

When I learned about OO, it was by teaching myself C++ first, a very painful process, and then I got around to reading about OO. The first thing I learned was that it was a matter of finding the nouns and then assigning verbs to the nouns. The nouns became classes and the verbs methods. This is the easy part, but it probably will yield only about 20 percent of the classes you will need.

If analysis leads to just the nouns and verbs described by the domain, then there will be a shortfall of classes, and much hacking will ensue. Beginning with the nouns and verbs of the domain is a good start, though.

Discovering More than Domain Analysis Yields

In addition to the things that your customers' experts tell you, you also will need to figure out how to make these things available to your customers and in almost all circumstances save the information that users provide. These pieces of information are referred to generically as *boundary, control*, and *entity classes*. A boundary class is a class used to connect elements outside the system with elements inside. Entity classes represent data. Typically, entities represent persisted data such as you might find in a database, and control classes manage or act on other classes. Users typically tell you a lot about entity classes and can help define GUIs based on how they complete tasks, but you have to work harder to find control and boundary classes.

TIP *If you ever work as an analyst, don't say, "You have told me about the entity classes; now tell me about the boundary classes." Analysis is an important task and probably should not be left to those with pencil protectors in their vest pockets. Interpersonal skills and a low-tech, conversational approach elicit a good exchange of ideas.*

An important perspective is to know that business experts will tell you a lot about the data they have to store, some about the processes they follow to get the data, and a little about a good way to get that data into a computer. A second important perspective is that users—the ones assigned to explain things to software engineers are called *domain experts*—may do a lot of things that don't make any sense to outsiders. From a rational point of view, this means that a process engineer may have never worked with his or her organization to examine what the organization does and how it does it and to determine if there is a better way to do it. The result is that you may get a lot of information that may not translate well to software—called a *low signal-to-noise ratio*—but the domain expert may feel it is important.

TIP *When it comes to analysis, the best advice I can offer is to buy an expensive pen and a leather-bound notebook, engage actively in the conversation, and take copious notes. In addition to users being flattered that so much lavish attention is being paid to them, it is difficult to know early in analysis what constitutes signal and what constitutes noise, so a lot of information is good.*

Having learned about the entity classes from users, your job is to figure out what the control and boundary classes are and how to model these things. The modeling is easiest, so let's start there.

Quite simply, an *entity class* is data and usually is long-lived or persisted, and entity classes can be modeled by adding the «entity» stereotype to the class symbol or using the entity class symbol available in many modeling tools (Figure 5-21). A *control class* is transient code that generally controls or acts on other classes and is responsible for transporting data between entity classes and boundary classes. Control classes are modeled by adding the «control» stereotype to a class or by using the class symbol (also shown in Figure 5-21). *Boundary classes* usually are found between subsystems. Boundary classes can be modeled as shown in Figure 5-21 or by adorning a class with the «boundary» stereotype.

A Nod to CRC Exercises

Class responsibility and collaborator (CRC) cards is a concept that involves a low-tech use of 3 × 5 index cards. The idea is that a group of interested people get

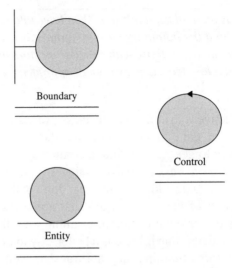

Figure 5-21   Rectangular class symbols and stereotypes can be replaced with symbols that specifically represent boundary, control, and entity classes.

together and write the classes they have discovered at the top of an index card. Underneath that they write a list of responsibilities, and adjacent to the responsibilities they write the class collaborators needed to support those responsibilities. If a card doesn't exist for a responsibility, then a new card is created.

The basic idea behind using small index cards is that they are too small to support a lot of behaviors, which is aimed at a reasonable division of responsibilities.

Creating CRC cards is a good idea, but you may want to get an expert to walk your group through it the first couple of times. Since that is practical advice but I can't stuff a CRC expert in this book, I will talk about alternatives, which are described in the next three subsections.

Finding Entity Classes

As I mentioned earlier, entity classes represent the data you will need to store. They also encompass logical entities. A logical entity is typically views or the result of heterogeneous queries, e.g.,

> select field1, field2 from customer, orders where order.customerid = customer.id

Simplistically, this query yields a result from customer and orders, which represents a logical customer orders entity.

Finding entities and logical entities is relatively easy because relational database theory is pretty well understood, and relational databases comprise a significantly recurring repository for entities. You will need entities for single tables and heterogeneous views comprised of multiple tables. From that point on, the entities are simply modeled as classes. You can use a «table» stereotype if the entities represent tables or no particular stereotype if you use custom classes.

Finding Control Classes

Control classes represent the bridge between entity classes and boundary classes and business logic in between. How you implement these classes depends on your implementation style. If you pick an implementation style, then finding entity classes can be derived from there.

Suppose that your implementation tool of choice predefines classes such as rows, tables, and datasets. If you elect to use your tool's classes, then your entity classes will be composed of those classes, and the classes that bridge to your entity classes will be defined by your tool's framework. On the other hand, if you pick custom entity classes, then your entity classes will be analogues to rows, tables, and datasets, but the control classes will still be framework classes that read and write to and from your persistence store, usually a database.

Control classes can mange how data are marshaled to entity classes, how data are marshaled to presentation classes, and how data are marshaled to other systems through boundary classes. There are many patterns that include general control patterns; the key is to recognize them. A famous pattern is called *model view controller* (MVC). In MVC, the model is represented by business objects, the GUI is your view, and control classes in between represent your controller. Implementing MVC or recognizing an implementation of MVC requires further study and practice. For example, Microsoft considers the ASP.NET pages in .NET to be an implementation of MVC. The ASPX or HTML page is the view, the controller is the code-behind page, and the model is the objects whose data are shown on the page. Implementing a custom MVC pattern in this context would be redundant. There are many books on patterns; *Design Patterns* (Reading, MA: Addison-Wesley, 1995) by Erich Gamma is a good place to start.

NOTE *There are many design patterns that can guide you when searching for boundary, control, and entity classes. A key here is to pick an implementation style and stick with it. You can compose a solution by finding entities first—called* database composition—*or by finding business objects—called* object composition—*or by designing GUIs first—called* presentation composition *or sometimes referred to as* hacking. *Any of these composition styles can be successful, but some styles work better than others depending on the size and complexity of the problem. Unfortunately, there is no single best style for all circumstances, and opinions vary greatly on this subject.*

Finding Boundary Classes

Boundary classes are used to bridge subsystems. The objective here is to insulate your system from direct interaction with external subsystems. In this way, if the external subsystem changes, your implementation will only need to change in the boundary classes. A good knowledge of patterns and a study of successful systems can help here.

This book is about the UML and is not intended to be a how-to book on software design. However, a scan of the Bibliography will lead you to some excellent books on UML and software design.

Quiz

1. The same basic symbol is used for interfaces and classes.

   a. True

   b. false

2. When adding classes to a diagram, you should

   a. show properties, fields, and methods.

   b. show properties and fields only.

   c. show properties and methods.

   d. show fields and methods.

3. An attribute can be modeled as a feature of a class but not as an association class.

   a. True

   b. False

4. When modeling attributes, it is

   a. required that you model attribute methods.

   b. recommended that you not show attribute methods.

   c. recommended that you show the underlying fields for those attributes.

   d. None of the above

5. Both simple types and complex types should be modeled as

   a. attributes.

   b. association classes.

    c. attributes and association classes.

    d. Simple types are best modeled as attributes, and complex types are best modeled as associations.

6. A unidirectional association has an arrow at one end called the source. The other end is called the target.

    a. The source will have a field whose type is the type of the target.

    b. The target will have a field whose type is the source.

    c. Neither

7. Are an aggregation and association

    a. semantically similar?

    b. directly opposite?

8. What is the most important difference between an aggregation and a composition?

    a. Composition means that the whole, or composite, class will be responsible for creating and destroying the part or contained class.

    b. Aggregation means that the whole aggregate class will be responsible for creating and destroying the part or contained class.

    c. Composition means that the whole, or composite, class is the only class that can have an instance of the part class at any given time.

    d. Aggregation means that the whole, or aggregate, class is the only class that can have an instance of the part class at any given time.

    e. a and c

    f. b and d

9. Generalization means

    a. polymorphism.

    b. association.

    c. inheritance.

    d. composition.

10. An association is named. The name is

    a. the type of the associated class.

    b. the implied name of the association and represents a field name.

    c. a dependency.

    d. a generalization.

11. The «primitive» is used in conjunction with the class symbol. It introduces
    a. existing simple types.
    b. new semantically simple types.
    c. existing complex types.
    d. new semantically complex types.

Answers

1. a
2. d
3. b
4. b
5. a
6. a
7. e
8. c
9. b
10. b
11. b

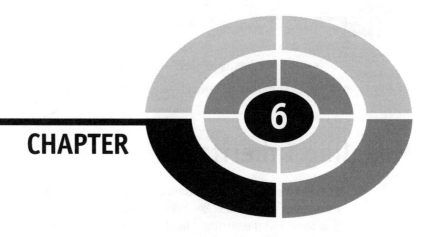

Showing How Classes Are Related

Chapter 5 introduced class diagrams as static views of your system. By *static view*, I mean that classes just lie there, but your classes define the things that are used to explore dynamic behaviors described in interaction diagrams and state charts.

Because classes and class diagrams contain elements central to your system, I will expand on the basic use of symbols and basic relationships from Chapter 5. This chapter will explore more advanced relationships and more detailed class information by looking at

- Diagrams with a greater number of elements
- Annotated relationships, including multiplicity
- Modeling abstract classes and interfaces

- Adding details to class diagrams
- Comparing classification to generalization

Modeling Inheritance

There are benefits to inheritance as well as challenges. A child class inherits all the features of its parent class. When an attribute is defined in a parent class, it is incorrect to repeat the attribute in child classes. If you repeat a method in a child class, then you are describing method overriding. In addition to overriding, you can redefine methods in the Unified Modeling Language (UML), and it is supported in some languages but can lead to confusion. Method overriding is central to polymorphism; use operation redefinition sparingly.

When you inherit classes, your child classes inherit the constraints defined by all ancestors. Each element has the union of the constraints it defines and constraints defined by its ancestors.

You have several inheritance options that I will explain in this section. This section will look at single inheritance and multiple inheritance and compare generalization with classification. To avoid deep inheritance trees, I also will explain interface inheritance and composition in the two sections that follow.

Using Single Inheritance

Single inheritance is the easiest form of inheritance. A child class that inherits from a parent class inherits all the features of the parent class but only has direct access to public and protected members. Inheritance, called *generalization* in the UML, is indicated by a single line extending from the child to the parent with a hollow triangle attached to the parent. If multiple classes inherit from the same parent, then you can use a single, merged line connecting to the parent.

Generalization versus Classification

In Chapter 5 I introduced an easy test to determine if an inheritance relationship exists. This is called the *is-a test*. This test alone can be misleading and result in incorrect results. Is-a implies strict transitivity. For example, if class B is a child of class A and class C is a child of class B, then class C is a child of class A. (We say that class C is a *grandchild* of class A or class A is an *ancestor* of class C.) However, the transitivity implied by the is-a test is not strictly correct.

Suppose that we have the following true statements:

Paul is a C# Programmer.
C# Programmer is a Job Description.
Paul is a Person.
C# Programmer is a Person.

"Paul is a C# Programmer" works. "A C# Programmer is a Person" works, and "C# Programmer is a Job Description" works, but "Paul is a Job Description" does not work. The problem is that Paul is an instance of C# Programmer. This relationship is described as a *classification* of Paul the C# Programmer, but generalization (i.e., inheritance) is used to describe relationships between subtypes. Therefore, be careful when using is-a as a sole determinant of inheritance. A more precise test is to determine if something describes an instance (classification) or a subtype (generalization).

If class B is a subtype of class A, then you have inheritance. If the relationship describes a classification—i.e., describes a context or role in which something is true—then you have a classification relationship. Classifications can be better managed with associations.

Dynamic Classification

The preceding discussion suggests that inheritance is sometimes misapplied. Returning to our example, Paul is-a programmer describes a role, or classification, more precisely than a generalization because Paul is also a husband, father, and taxpayer. If we tried to generalize Paul as all those things through inheritance, we'd have to use multiple inheritance, and the relationships would be pretty complex.

The way to model and capture classification is through association. In fact, we can use a state behavior pattern to capture the dynamic and changing roles that describe a person or how the instance Paul behaves in a given context. Using association and, more specifically, the state behavior pattern, we can implement dynamic classification. That is, we can change Paul's behavior based on the context or the role he is playing at a given moment.

The *state behavior pattern* is implemented using an association and generalization. Without trying to reproduce the entire discussion on this pattern—refer to *Design Patterns*, by Erich Gamma et al.—we can summarize. The state behavior pattern is called a *behavior* pattern because it is a pattern that describes how something acts. The other general kinds of patterns are *creational*—how something is created—and *structural*—how something is organized. The pattern is named the *state* pattern because it describes how something behaves based on state. In our example, we would use this pattern to describe how people behave based on some condition, the state. For example, when Paul is at work, he behaves like a C# programmer. When Paul is at home, he behaves like a husband when interacting with his wife and a father when interacting with his children.

If we incorrectly modeled the classification of Paul using generalization, then we would create a model that looked like Figure 6-1 showing all inheritance. However, if we modeled Paul's roles more precisely using association, we would have a better model (see Figure 6-2).

Figure 6-1 tries to show that a "Person" is an instance of "Programmer," "Husband," and "Father." In reality, this implies that a different kind of object would have to be created for Paul depending on context. In reality, however, Paul is always a person, and people have roles. Sometimes a person is a spouse. Sometimes a person is a parent. Sometimes a person is a worker, and so on. The association role means that Paul is always an instance of a "Person," but a person's role changes dynamically. The italicized class *"Role"* means that role is abstract, and the association (lowercase) "role" is actually an instance of "C# Programmer," "Husband," or "Father."

The state behavior pattern is implemented mostly by the relationship between "Person" and the abstract class *"Role."* What is missing to complete the pattern are abstract behaviors that need to be defined by person and implemented by generalizations of role. For example, "Person" could have a method called "ExercisePatience," and that method would be declared in *"Role"* and implemented by calling "role." "ExercisePatience," i.e., "Person's" behavior named "ExercisePatience," would be implemented by a specific subclass of "Role." For instance, in the "C# Programmer" role if you yell at customers, then you may lose your job, but yelling at your spouse

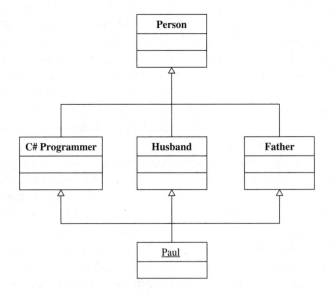

Figure 6-1 A UML class diagram showing a rigid generalization where the object "Paul" is trying to incorrectly reflect "Father," "Husband," and "C# Programmer."

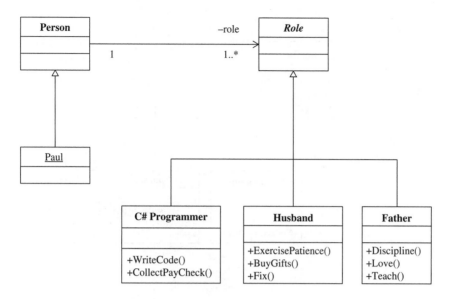

Figure 6-2   A second UML class diagram that uses association to a role reflecting how people behave in certain roles.

may result in your sleeping on the couch. The specific role subtype determines the behavior without changing the "Person" instance.

NOTE *In today's complex society, modeling familial relationships, e.g., for state government, could be exceedingly difficult. Children have multiple parents, sometimes the gender of both parents is identical, and some people have multiple jobs and nuclear families. However, this illustrates that something as seemingly simply as people and their roles can be very complex depending on the problem domain.*

If gender suited our design context, then we could further classify "Husband" and "Father" as having an association with an enumeration, "Gender" (Figure 6-3). The key is not to model everything you could model; instead, model what you need to model to describe the problem suitably enough for your problem space.

Using Multiple Inheritance

Single inheritance can be hard because the is-a test isn't completely sufficient. Generalization implies subtype, but you could implement subtype relationships using composition or association. Single inheritance is additionally challenging because classification means that you are talking about an instance, and is-a seems to work during verbal discussions but may be incorrect or too rigid to implement.

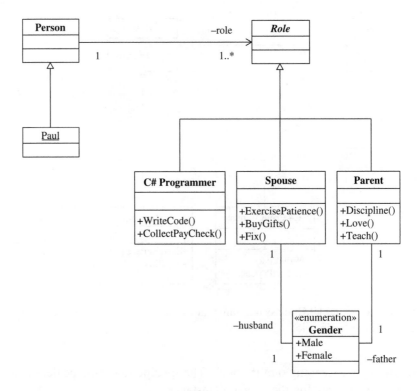

Figure 6-3 Abstracting gender from the roles of spouse and parent.

Multiple inheritance is even more difficult because we still have generalization and classification problems, and these are exacerbated by having more than one supertype. When a subtype inherits from more than one supertype, the subtype is understood to contain the union of all the features of all the subtype's parents. So far so good. A problem occurs when more than one supertype introduces a feature that has the same name as another supertype. For instance, class C inherits from class B and class A, and both class A and class B introduce an operation named "Foo." Which version of "Foo" does "C.Foo()" resolve to, "A.Foo()" or "B.Foo()"? Although the UML supports dynamic conflict resolution, most implementations of multiple inheritance require the programmer to resolve the conflict. This means that the programmer has to decide that "C.Foo()" calls "A.Foo()," "B.Foo()," or both "A.Foo()" and "B.Foo()" (Figure 6-4). A good practice when using multiple inheritance is to resolve name conflicts explicitly.

Multiple inheritance is indicated when a class has more than one immediate supertype. The movie *Chitty Chitty Bang Bang* was produced by Albert Broccoli and Ian Fleming, the same pair who produced the James Bond flicks. In the movie, the car also was a water-jet-propulsed hydrofoil and an airplane. In a class diagram,

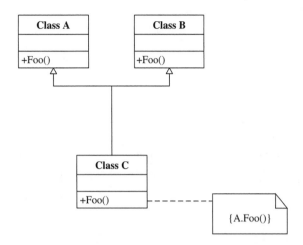

Figure 6-4   Resolve name conflicts in classes with multiple inheritance explicitly, shown here using a constraint.

this could be modeled as a class (we'll call it "CCBB") inheriting from "Boat," "Automobile," and "Airplane." The problem arises because each mode used a different form of propulsion; consequently, "CCBB.Propulse()" might be hard to resolve in a model and equally difficult to implement.

NOTE   *You might think that amphibious vehicles and the verb* propulse *a bit of a stretch, but from real experience, I can tell you that such concepts presently exist in designs. However, I am only aware of actual examples in military applications.*

Because of real technical difficulties with multiple inheritance, many powerful languages, such as C# and Java, do not support the idiom. Another reason multiple inheritance is not universally supported is that you can simulate multiple inheritance through composition and constituent feature promotion or through multiple-interface inheritance. From the UML's perspective, composition and surfacing constituent features mean that "CCBB" would be a car and would have plane and boat objects contained within, and the features of boat and plane would be made available indirectly by redefining features at the car level. These features then would be implemented by invoking the internally composited boat or plane features. For example, "CCBB.Fly" would invoke the internal "Plane.Fly" method. Multiple-interface inheritance means simply that a class will implement all the features defined by all the realized interfaces.

Avoid multiple inheritance even if it is supported in your implementation language of choice, and use composition or interface inheritance instead. Figure 6-5

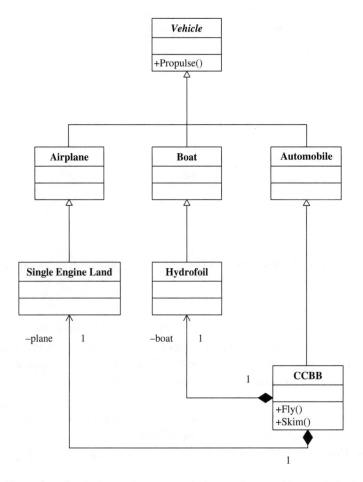

Figure 6-5   In this figure we show that "CCBB" inherits from "Automobile" but uses composition to show its boat- and planelike capabilities.

shows one way that we could draw a class diagram to depict CCBB's aerodynamic and amphibian features. In the figure, we understand the diagram to mean that "CCBB" creates an instance of "Hydrofoil" named "boat" and an instance of "Single Engine Land Aircraft" named "plane." "Skim()" would be implemented by calling "boat.Propulse," and "Fly()" would be implemented by calling "plane.Propulse."

Another option would be to define three interfaces: "Airplane," "Automobile," and "Boat." Each of these interfaces could define methods, "Fly," "Drive," and "Propel." Then "CCBB" could implement each of these interfaces.

The solution shown in Figure 6-5 is not perfect, and it may not appeal to everyone. However, it is important to keep in mind that what we are striving for with models is *good enough* or *attainable*, not perfect.

Modeling Interface Inheritance

There are three primary activities associated with modeling. Modelers have to figure out a solution to problems quickly and often in group situations. Modelers have to use UML tools, and this is often done by one person in isolation or a smaller group, and finally, some supporting text documentation generally is requested. Writing architectural documentation is beyond the scope of this book, but group modeling on napkins and whiteboards and using UML tools are both important. Sometimes I think whiteboards and napkins are more important than UML tools because group modeling involves more people, and I am not completely convinced that actual UML models are read by anyone other than the modelers and programmers and only the programmers occasionally.

Whiteboarding

Drawing models on a whiteboard can be convenient because it is easy to do, and you can get feedback from the observing group and change the drawing. However, if you try to use the formality and features found in UML tools on a whiteboard, you get bogged down in drawing pretty pictures rather than solving problems. For this reason, it is acceptable to use shorthand notations and smaller symbols, and it is okay if your rectangles aren't perfect on a whiteboard.

For example, in the UML, we use italics to indicate that a class is abstract. On a whiteboard, we can use an abbreviation for the keyword abstract (A) to mean that a class is abstract. Instead of writing the stereotype «interface» for interfaces, we can use «I» or the lollipop. Suppose that we were discussing properties of flight in a group setting. We could define an interface "IFlyable" with methods "GetDrag," "GetLift," "GetThrust," and "GetWeight" and show that a parachute implements these operations (although it is very hard to simulate a whiteboard in a book). Figure 6-6 shows how we might render the UML on a whiteboard, and Figure 6-7 shows the same UML captured in our modeling tool.

Figure 6-7 is neater and better than UML, but many modelers, especially those with just a little exposure to UML, will recognize that the two renderings represent the same solution. Additionally, simply explaining what the lollipop is will satisfy novices and is much easier to draw on a whiteboard.

Note *"Lift," "Drag," "Weight," and "Thrust" are the values needed for the principles of flight described by the physics of Bernoulli and Newton. These properties actually came into play when I was discussing solutions for a peer-to-peer networked collision-avoidance system for high-speed parachutes for high-altitude, or Halo, jumpers.*

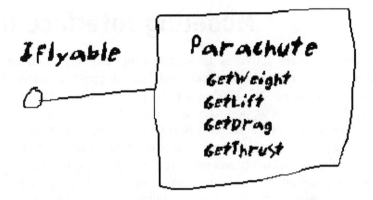

Figure 6-6 The interface "IFlyable" shown realized by "Parachute," as we might draw it on a whiteboard.

The point is that in a dynamic group situation, it is helpful to be quick because a lot of information may be thrown out, sometimes all at once. Using a shorthand notation may not always yield perfect UML, but the language is a tool for understanding and solving problems and is the means not the end. You always can draw pretty UML when the meeting is over.

Using Realization

If generalization is overused, then realization is probably underused. *Realization* means interface inheritance, and it is indicated by using a class with the «interface» stereotype and a connector with a dashed line connected to a hollow triangle. The triangle is attached to the interface, and the other end is attached to the class that will implement the interface.

The lollipop symbol handdrawn in Figure 6-6 is still used by some modeling tools and is a recognizable shorthand along with a solid-line connector for interface inheritance. The difficulty in using multiple symbols to mean the same thing is that it makes a language harder to understand and, if used imprecisely, may lead

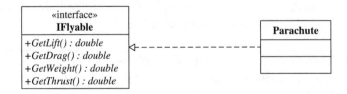

Figure 6-7 The same diagram as shown in Figure 6-6 rendered in Visio.

to language lawyering by UML weenies. Language lawyering is almost always a waste of time except by academics.

Provider Relationships and Required Relationships

In the UML, the lollipop actually is used to show relationships between interfaces and classes. The lollipop means that the attached class provides the interface. A half-lollipop or line with a semicircle means that an interface is required. If we apply the symbols for provider and required relationships to our parachute example, then we can model our high-speed parachutes as providing "IFlyable" (on the left) and requiring "INavigable" on the right (Figure 6-8).

In Figure 6-8, the parachute itself has properties of flight, including "Lift," "Thrust," "Drag," and "Weight," even though "Thrust" is probably 0, but a navigable parachute may depend on a GPS (Global Positioning System) device that knows about longitude and latitude and an altimeter that knows about altitude (and wind speed and direction). We also could show the identical relationship using the realization connector for "IFlyable" and the dependency connector for "INavigable" (Figure 6-9). If you are interested in emphasizing the relationships, then you can use lollipops; if you want to emphasize the operations, then the class symbol with the stereotypes is a better choice.

Rules for Interface Inheritance

The basic idea behind interfaces is that an interface describes behavioral specification without providing behaviors, such as navigability. In our parachute example, we are only saying that our high-speed collision-avoiding parachutes will interact with a device that acts as an aid to navigation, perhaps by increasing drag. The presence of the interface does not dictate what the device is; it only dictates the behaviors the device supports.

TIP *Using an adjective—e.g.,* attribute *becomes* attributable—*for interface names is a common practice. Sometimes a good dictionary comes in handy.*

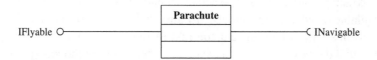

Figure 6-8   "IFlyable" is an interface provided by "Parachute," and "INavigable" shows an interface required by "Parachute."

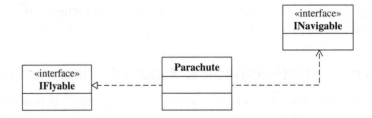

Figure 6-9 This figure depicts the same relationships as those described in Figure 6-8, specifically, that "Parachute" realizes "IFlyable" and depends on "INavigable."

Interfaces do not provide behaviors; they only stipulate what they must be. The rule is that an interface must be implemented through realization or inheritance. This means that

- Given interface A, class B can implement all the behaviors described by interface A.

- Given interface A and interface B, which inherits from interface A, class C can implement all the behaviors described by interfaces A and B.

- Given interface A and classes B and C, where class C inherits from class B or class B is composed of class C, together classes B and C implement all the behaviors described by interface A. In the composition scenario, B realizes A, and in the inheritance scenario, C realizes A.

Assuming that "INavigable's" behavioral specification included "GetLongitude()," "GetLatitude()," and "GetAltitude()," then "INavigable" in the first scenario could be realize by a device that can determine longitude, latitude, and altidude. In the second scenario, "INavigable" might inherit from an interface "IAltitudinal," and both interfaces are realized by a single three-dimensionally orienting device. Finally, in the third scenario, "INavigable" might define all three-dimensional positions and be implemented by generalization or composition, as shown in Figure 6-10. (Just to satisfy my curiosity, such a device does exist—the Garmin eTrex Summit GPS with Electronic Compass and Altimeter. I want one.)

Again, it is worth noting that the three scenarios described all satisfy the requirement of navigability adequately. The actual scenario I design depends on what classes I have available or what is convenient. If I already have part of the interface realized by another class, then I might get the rest through inheritance of composition. Remember that the design doesn't have to be perfect, but the models should describe what you mean adequately. You always can change your mind if you have to.

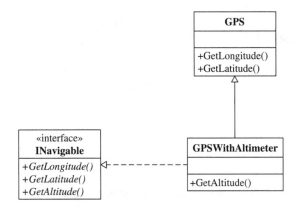

Figure 6-10   Implementing an interface through inheritance.

Describing Aggregation and Composition

Aggregation gets a mention here because it is the term most often used in object-oriented software design when talking about composition, i.e., when talking about one class being composed of others. *Aggregation* is the term used, but *composition* is what is meant. As I said earlier, the aggregation connector—composed of a hollow diamond and a solid line—has an ambiguous meaning that is no different from an association, and association is preferred.

Composition uses a solid diamond and a solid line. When you use composition, it means that the class that represents the whole, or composite class, contains the one and only instance of the class representing the part; it also means that the whole class is responsible for the lifetime of the part class.

Composition means that the composite class must ensure that all its parts are created and attached to the composite before the composite is wholly constructed. As long as the composite exists, it can be implemented to rely on none of its parts being destroyed by any other entity. When the composite is destroyed, it must destroy the parts, or it can explicitly remove parts and hand them off to some other object. The multiplicity of the composite is always 1 or 0.1.

To demonstrate composition, we can modify the relationship illustrated in Figure 6-10. In this figure I demonstrated how to satisfy an interface through inheritance, but the name of the child class, "GPSWithAltimeter," sounds like a composition relationship. The word *with* suggests composition to me more than it suggests inheritance. In order to satisfy the interface, we can define "GPSWithAlitimeter" as the composite, define "Altimeter" as the part, and promote the "GetAltitude" method

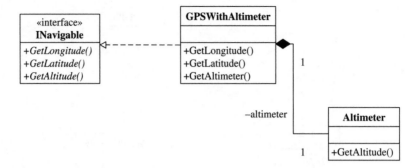

Figure 6-11 Figure 6-10 revised to use composition to add the behavior of the altimeter.

from "Altimeter." Figure 6-11 shows the revision, and the listing that follows shows how we might stub each of these elements in C#.

```csharp
public interface INavigable
{

        double GetLongitude();
  double GetLatitude();
  double GetAltitude();
}

public class Altimeter
{

            /// <summary>
  /// Return meters MSL (mean sea level)
  /// </summary>
  /// <returns></returns>
  public double GetAltitude()
  {
    return 0;
  }
}

public class GPSWithAltimeter : INavigable
{
  private Altimeter altimeter;

  public GPSWithAltimeter()
  {
    altimeter = new Altimeter();
  }
```

```
#region INavigable Members

public double GetLongitude()
{
  return 0;
}

public double GetLatitude()
{
  return 0;
}

public double GetAltitude()
{
  return altimeter.GetAltitude();
}

#endregion
}
```

In this listing we can see that "GPSWithAltimeter" contains a private field "altimeter." The constructor creates an instance of the altimeter, and "GetAltitude" uses the altimeter to return the altitude. Because C# is a "garbage collected" language, we do not have to show a destructor explicitly releasing the instance of the altimeter part. (Now all that is left to do is implement the behaviors.)

Showing Associations and Association Classes

Chapter 5 introduced the association. Let's take a moment to recap, and then I will introduce some advanced concepts relative to associations.

When you see a field in a class, that is an association. However, an association in a class diagram often is limited to classes rather than simple types. For example, an array of cardinal values could be shown as an array field or an association to the type cardinal with a multiplicity of 1 on the end representing the class that contains the array and a multiplicity of many (*) on the cardinal type. In addition, fields and associations support navigability, changeability, and ordering. That same array of cardinal types could be represented by attaching the stick arrow connected to the type cardinal. If we wanted to indicate that the array was read-only—perhaps after initialization—then we could place the modifier {read only} on the field and on the association. The meaning is the same. If the array were ordered, then we could

Figure 6-12 We can add modifiers and details to associations just as we would add them to fields.

place the {ordered} modifier on the array field or on the association. Figure 6-12 shows our array of cardinal values represented using a directed association of ordered (sorted) cardinal values.

If an association has features, then we can use an association class. Think of an association class as a linking table in a relational database, but it is a linking table with behaviors. For example, we can indicate that an "Employer" is associated with its "Employees." If we wanted to indicate that "Employees" is a collection that can be ordered, then we can add an association class called "EmployeeList" and show the "Sort" method in that class (Figure 6-13).

In our example, we can elect to use an association to reflect that employers and employees are associated rather than an employer being a composite composed of employees. This also works nicely because many people have more than one employer.

An association class is a class that has an association connector attached to an association between the classes it links. In the example, the class "Employer" would have a field whose type is "EmployeeList," and "EmployeeList" has a method "Sort" and is associated with (or contains) the "Employee" objects. If we left the "EmployeeList" linking class out of the model and still maintained the one-to-many

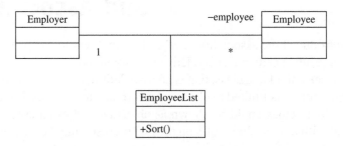

Figure 6-13 An association class showing that the class "EmployeeList" links "Employer" to "Employees" indirectly.

relationship, then it would be assumed that some sort of collection exists, but the programmer would be free to devise this relationship. The linking class clarifies the relationship more precisely.

We also could model the relationship using by association the "Employer" to the "EmployeeList" and the "EmployeeList" to the "Employee." The diagram in Figure 6-14 shows three variations on basically the same thing.

The topmost part of Figure 6-14 implies an array or collection and, with simple instructions, such as *"Use a typed collection of Employee objects,"* is often sufficient for a proper implementation. The bottom two diagrams in Figure 6-14 provide slightly more information and indicate ownership of the sorting behavior, but the implementation of any of the three figures should be almost identical.

Suppose further that we elected to show how a specific employee was accessed from the collection by a type, perhaps an employee identification number. For example, given an employee identification number, we could indicate that an employee identification number results in a unique employee. This is called a *qualified association* and can be modeled by adding the class of the qualifier, as shown in Figure 6-15.

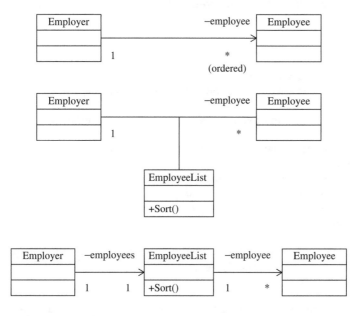

Figure 6-14   Three variations that reflect a one-to-many relationship between an "Employer" and "Employees."

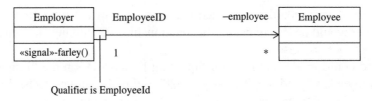

Qualifier is EmployeeId

Figure 6-15 The qualifier that yields a unique employee is the "EmployeeId."

When you see a qualifier, you will expect to see the qualifier used as a parameter that yields a specific instance of the associated type. The code listing that follows shows how we can implement this code in Visual Basic.NET using a typed collection of "Employee" objects, a class named "EmployeeId," and an indexer.

```vbnet
Imports System.Collections

Public Class Employer
    Private employees As EmployeeList

    Public Sub New()
        employees = New EmployeeList
    End Sub

End Class

Public Class EmployeeList
    Inherits System.Collections.CollectionBase

    Default Public Property Item(ByVal id As EmployeeID) As Employee
        Get
            Return GetEmployee(id)
        End Get
        Set(ByVal Value As Employee)
            SetEmployee(Value, id)
        End Set
    End Property

    Public Function Add(ByVal value As EmployeeList) As Integer
        Return List.Add(value)
    End Function

    Private Function Indexof(ByVal value As EmployeeID) As Integer
        Dim i As Integer
        For i = 1 To List.Count
            If (CType(List(i), Employee).ID.IsEqual(value)) Then
                Return i
            End If
        Next
```

```vb
            Throw New IndexOutOfRangeException("id not found")
    End Function

    Private Function GetEmployee(ByVal id As EmployeeID) As Employee
        Return List(Indexof(id))
    End Function

    Private Sub SetEmployee(ByVal value As Employee, _
      ByVal id As EmployeeID)
        List(Indexof(id)) = value
    End Sub
End Class


Public Class Employee
    Private FName As String
    Private FID As EmployeeId

    Public Property Name() As String
        Get
            Return FName
        End Get
        Set(ByVal Value As String)
            FName = Value
        End Set
    End Property

    Public Property ID() As EmployeeID
        Get
            Return FID
        End Get
        Set(ByVal Value As EmployeeID)
            FID = Value
        End Set
    End Property
End Class


Public Class EmployeeID
    Private ssn As String

    Public Sub New(ByVal value As String)
        ssn = value
    End Sub

    Public Function IsEqual(ByVal value As EmployeeID) As Boolean
        Return value.ssn.ToUpper() = ssn.ToUpper()
    End Function
End Class
```

Even if you are unfamiliar with Visual Basic.NET, you can look at the class headers and see all the classes shown in Figure 6-15 (which includes "Employer,"

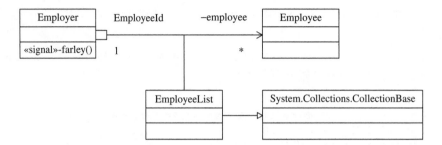

Figure 6-16   The revised diagram uses an association class to introduce the generalization that shows that "EmployeeList" inherits from "System.Collections.CollectionBase."

"Employee," "EmployeeId," and the implied "EmployeeList"). [The fact that "EmployeeList" inherits from "System.Collections.CollectionBase" is specialized knowledge that is required in any particular language or framework. You have the option of showing the generalization of "CollectionBase" by "EmployeeList," which you could add to the diagram (Figure 6-16) if your developers needed a little extra hand holding.]

The deciding factor that helps me to choose how much detail to add is my programmer audience. If my programmer partners are very experienced in the implementation language and framework of choice, then I might leave off details about how to implement the collection of employees. For new programmers, it may be helpful to show the added information in Figure 6-16. In practice, with very new programmers I usually add more detail and then code an exemplar that shows them how to implement the construct, in this case a typed collection specific to Visual Basic.NET.

___

NOTE   *Even detailed UML diagrams aren't always clear to everyone. For this reason, it is often an important detail that modelers know how to implement the diagrams they create in the target platform chosen or at least that one person on the team can translate advanced aspects of the UML diagrams into code.*

Exploring Dependency Relationships

A *dependency* is a relationship of client and supplier also referred to as *source* and *target*. The dependency relationship is a dashed line with a stick arrow at the end. The arrow is attached to the supplier, also called the *target*. I prefer the term *source*, and *target* as target makes it easier to remember which end the arrow points to.

A dependency in a class diagram means that the source is dependent on the target in some way. If the target changes, then the source is affected. This means that if the target's interface changes, then implementation of the source will be affected. Dependencies are not transitive. For instance, if class A is dependent on class B and class B is dependent on class C, then if class C's interface changes, class B's implementation may have to change but not necessarily class B's interface. However, if dependencies are cyclic—class A depends on class B depends on class C depends on class A—then changes to class C can have a cyclic effect that makes changes very difficult, resulting in a brittle implementation. As a general rule, avoid complicated and cyclic dependencies.

Directed associations, composition, and inheritance imply a dependency. If class A has a directed association with class B, then class A is dependent on class B. If class B inherits from class A, then class B is dependent on class A. Association and generalization are more precise relationships with their own connotations; use dependency when one of the more specific kinds of relationships doesn't apply.

Finally, before we explore some of the predefined stereotypes that apply to dependencies, don't try to show all dependency relationships. Just draw the dependencies that are important.

Table 6-1 shows the predefined stereotypes for dependencies. Often the implication of a dependency is clear by its context, but these stereotypes exist to clearly

access	Private reference to another package's contents.
bind	Describes a new element that is created when the template parameter is assigned.
call	A method in the source calls a method in the target.
create	The source creates an instance of the target.
derive	One object is derived from another.
instantiate	The source creates an instance of the target.
permit	The source can access the target's private members (e.g., implemented as a friend relationship in some languages).
realize	The source implements the interface of the target. (The realization connector is a better choice.)
refine	The source refines the target. This is used for traceability between models (e.g., between an analysis and design model).
send	Indicates a sender and receiver of a signal.
substitute	The source can be substituted for the target. (This is similar to how a subclass can be substituted for its superclass.)
trace	Used to link model elements.
use	The source needs the target to complete its implementation.

Table 6-1 A List of Stereotypes for Dependency Relationships Defined by the UML Version 2.0

state your intended use. (Following the table is a brief description of each of the dependency relationships.)

Often it is enough to draw the occasional dependency connector in code and implement what you mean. The following paragraphs elaborate on some of the dependency relationships described in Table 6-1.

The "access" dependency supports importing packages privately. Some of these concepts are new in UML version 2.0, and this is one I haven't had occasion to use. The closest example that might apply here is the difference between the interface and implementation use clauses in Delphi. Essentially, Delphi supports private importation in its implementation use clauses.

If you have ever read *The C++ Programming Language*, by Bjarne Stroustrop, then you would have read the discourse on template classes. In C with classes, templates originated as a weakly typed construct devised by using substitution and macros. The result was that the new name created by concatenating the string type resulted in a new class. With templates, the result is the same. When you define the parameter for parameterized types—templates or generics—you have a new entity. "Bind" exists for purposes of modeling this occurrence.

"Call" straightforwardly calls a method of the target class. "Create" indicates that the source creates an instance of the target. You might see this relationship in conjunction with the factory pattern. A factory's sole purpose is to perform all the steps necessary to create the correct object.

"Derive," "realize," "refine," and "trace" are abstract dependencies. They exist to represent two versions of the same thing. For example, the "realize" dependency implies the same relationship as a realization—i.e., the implementation of an interface. "Trace" is used to connect model elements as they evolve, e.g., use cases to use case realizations.

"Instantiate" also might be used to indicate that the source creates instances of the target. A better example has to do with runtime type information or reflection in .NET. We could show that a metaclass (or the an instance of the "Type" object in .NET) is used to create an instance of a class.

The "permit" stereotype is used to indicate that the source can invoke nonpublic members of the target. This relationship is supported by the "Friend" modifier in languages such as Visual Basic and through dynamic reflection.

A *signal* is like an event that occurs out of sequence. For example, when you are asleep and your alarm begins to ring, this is a signal to wake up. The "signal" stereotype is used to indicate that something has happened that needs a response. Think event.

The "substitute" stereotype applies when the source can be substituted with the target. The clearest form of substitution is a child class in place of a parent. Finally, the "use" stereotype is common. "Use" simply implies that the source needs the target to be complete. "Use" is a more generalized form of "call," "create," "instantiate," and "send."

Adding Details to Classes

The devil is in the details, as they say. Class diagrams can include a lot of information that is conveyed by text characters, fonts, and what is included, as well as what is excluded. I prefer to be explicit to the extent possible but not verbose and to be personally present to resolve ambiguities during implementation. In this section I want to point out a few details that you can look for and some respectable shortcuts you can take to ensure that you understand UML diagrams created by others and that others understand your diagrams. Because these basic guidelines are relatively short, they are listed as statements.

- Underlined features indicate static features.

- Derived properties are demarked by a slash preceding the property name. For example, given properties "hours worked" and "hourly wage," we can derive the wage, which would appear as "/wage."

- Italicized class names indicate abstract classes. An abstract class has some elements with no implementation and depends on subclasses for a complete implementation.

- Model fields; properties are implied in languages that support properties. In languages that don't support properties, methods prefixed with "get_" and "set_" yield the same result.

- Constraints specify before (pre) and after (post) conditions. Use constraints to indicate the state in which an object should be when a method is entered and a method is exited. The "assertion" construct supports this style of programming.

- When you are modeling operations, try to maintain a minimum number of public operations, use private fields, and permit access to fields through properties (if supported) or accessor methods (if properties are not supported).

Quiz

1. A subclass has access to a superclass's private members.
    a. True
    b. False

2. If a child class has more than one parent and each parent introduces an operation with the same name,

   a. the programmer should resolve the name conflict explicitly.

   b. all languages that support multiple inheritance resolve conflicts implicitly.

   c. Neither of the above. Conflicts are not allowed.

3. Which of the following statements is (are) true?

   a. Generalization refers to subtypes.

   b. Classification refers to subtypes.

   c. Generalization refers to object instances.

   d. Classification refers to object instances.

   e. None of the above

4. To realize

   a. means to inherit from a parent class.

   b. means to implement an interface.

   c. means to promote the constituent members in a composite class.

   d. is a synonym for aggregation.

5. If a language does not support multiple inheritance, then the result can be approximated by

   a. an association and the promotion of constituent properties.

   b. realization.

   c. composition and the promotion of constituent properties.

   d. aggregation and the promotion of constituent properties.

6. Dynamic classification—where an object is changed at runtime—can be modeled using

   a. generalization.

   b. association.

   c. realization.

   d. composition.

7. An "association" class is referred to as a linking class.

   a. True

   b. False

8. An "association" qualifier

    a. is used as a precondition to an association.

    b. plays the role of a parameter used to return a unique object.

    c. is used as a post condition to an association.

    d. is the same thing as a directed association.

9. Pick the correct statements.

    a. A provided interface means that a class implements an interface.

    b. A required interface means that a class depends on an interface.

    c. A provided interface means that a class depends on an interface.

    d. A required interface means that a class implements an interface.

10. When a classifier symbol is italicized,

    a. it means that the symbol represents an object.

    b. it means that the symbol represents an abstract class.

    c. it means that the symbol represents an interface.

    d. it means that the symbol is a derived value.

Answers

1. b
2. a
3. a and d
4. b
5. c
6. b
7. a
8. b
9. a and b
10. b

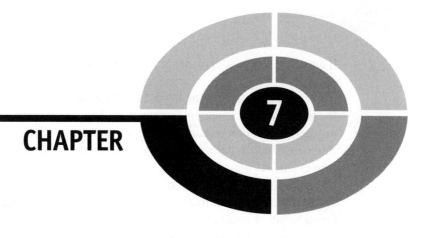

Using State Chart Diagrams

Historically, the difference between state charts and activity diagrams was muddled. In the Unified Modeling Language (UML) version 2.0, state charts come into their own as a distinct and separate diagram.

State charts (also known as *state machines*) are good at showing an object's state over many use cases and good at defining protocols that describe a correct orchestration of messages, such as might be needed for database access or Transmission Control Protocol (TCP) connectivity. State charts are ideally suited for describing the behavior of user interfaces and device controllers for real-time systems. Whereas interaction diagrams are good at understanding systems, state charts are good at indicating behavior precisely. If you are working in real-time systems or with physical device controllers, then you may use state charts frequently. However, a huge number of applications are business applications based on graphical user interfaces (and databases and many programmers use modern rapid application development tools to prototype interfaces rather than define their behaviors using state charts).

[I am not making a judgment about whether prototypes should be created without state charts, but prototyping graphical user interfaces (GUIs) is not part of the UML.]

Part of demystifying the UML is making sure that you know that you don't need to use every model element, create every kind of diagram, or model every aspect of a system. Stick to modeling elements that are complicated and where model exploration may lead to a better solution. For example, if you are using a well-understood framework such as ADO.NET, it is unnecessary to create protocol diagrams that show how to open a connection, read data, and close a connection. These processes are prescribed by the framework, and time spent creating the model is time that could be better spent elsewhere. This said, occasionally you will want or need state charts, and in this chapter I will show you the elements of state charts and some examples. You will learn

- About the elements used to create state charts

- How to create state charts

- The difference between behavioral and protocol state charts

- Common ways to implement state charts

Elements of a State Diagram

The simplest thing about the UML is that most diagrams are composed of simple symbols and lines. This is true of state charts, which are composed significantly of symbols called *states* and lines called *transitions*. The simplicity of the symbols is the easiest part of modeling; identifying problems, grasping solutions, and capturing this understanding are the aspects of UML modeling that can make modeling as complex as programming.

Three things to remember are

- Knowing all the tokens and grammar does not imply that you have to use them all.

- It is important to model the important aspects of the system and to model those that aren't obvious.

- You don't need every kind of diagram for every kind of problem; be selective.

This said, let's expand our knowledge of the UML and look at the various symbols for state charts that evolved from their interspersed relationship with activity diagrams.

Exploring State Symbols

There are several state symbols. The most common is the rounded rectangle, or simple state. Significantly state charts consist of simple states and transitions, but there are other states that play important though less prominent roles.

In this section I will explain simple states with regular and do activities; orthogonal and nonorthogonal composite states; initial, terminate, and final states; junctions, choices, and history states; submachine states; and superstates, exit, and entry points.

Using Initial, Final, and Terminate States

Recall that state charts and activity diagrams have a shared history. Consequently, although their definitions in the UML version 2.0 are more clearly delineated, state charts and activity diagrams still share some symbols in common. Three states, initial, final, and terminal, use the same symbols found in activity diagrams but play roles tailored to state charts.

The initial state is a solid circle representing a pseduostate in protocol state machines—see "Creating Protocol State Machines" below—in the UML version 2.0. You can use the initial state in state charts in general, but it is not used commonly. The final state uses the same symbol—a solid circle with a circular outline—as the final activity in activity diagrams and is used to indicate the end of a state chart—see "Creating Behavioral State Machines" below. Final states don't have outgoing transitions; don't have entry, exit, or do activities; don't reference submachines; and aren't divided into regions. (These concepts are described in a moment.) The final state is an endpoint without elaboration. The terminate state is an X used in protocol state machines; think of it as a dead end.

Using Junction and Choice States

A choice state is a pseudostate that is used in protocol state machines. A choice looks like a decision diamond and plays a similar role to a decision in activity diagrams. A choice has a single incoming transition and has more than one outgoing transition. Outgoing transitions are taken depending on which guard condition evaluates to true. If more than one guard evaluates to true, then an arbitrary transition is taken, but at least one guard must evaluate to true (Figure 7-1).

A junction is a solid circle, like the initial state, and is used to merge several incoming transitions into a single outgoing transition or split a single incoming transition into multiple outgoing transitions (Figure 7-2).

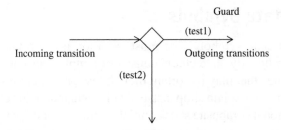

Figure 7-1 A choice state showing a single incoming transition and two outgoing transitions, each with a guard condition.

The biggest problem with using older-style notations and symbols is that if you try to generate code, the tool probably will report an error. However, the state of code generators is still iffy, and each tool has some limitations relative to the formal specification of the UML.

Because of a state chart's shared history with activity diagrams, you might see junctions modeled using the fork and join symbols employed in activity diagrams. Both the fork/join and junction with their incoming and outgoing transitions clearly indicate the intent of transitions splitting or merging.

Using Shallow and Deep History States

A shallow history is indicated by a circle with an H, and a deep history is indicated by a circle with an H*. Histories are used in protocol state machines. A shallow history is used to represent a recent substate for a composite state, and a deep history is used to represent a recursive history of substates. (Refer to the upcoming section on composite states for more information.)

If a state machine transitions to a history state, then the most recent state is activated and executed. Think of history states as a means of modeling undo, redo, or

Figure 7-2 A junction showing multiple incoming transitions with a single outgoing transition.

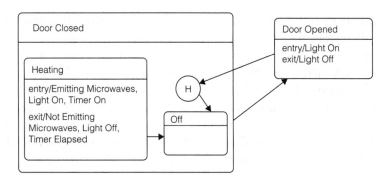

Figure 7-3   A composite state showing a shallow history—circle H—indicating that the state of the microwave is stored when the door is opened.

pause and resume behaviors. Figure 7-3 shows a composite state—see "Using Composite States" below—representing a microwave oven. When the door is closed, we could be heating, or the oven just could be off. When we are heating, a timer, a light, and the microwave emitter are on; when we exit the heating mode, the timer, the light, and the emitter are off. If the door is opened, then the light is on, and a history is stored before we transition to the OFF state. The history is intended to permit resuming at the elapsed timer point if we start the oven again.

In the early part of the last century it was discovered that microwaves could be bounced off objects and used to detect direction and range. The original application was intended to detect German Messerschmitts during World War II. Dr. Percy Spencer at Raytheon accidentally discovered that the microwave emitter melted some chocolate in his pocket. Spencer tried some popcorn kernels in a paper bag next, and the microwave oven was discovered. Owing to its original application as radar, the oven was called the "radar range," and eventually the name was changed to *microwave oven*. The first radar range was 6 feet high and cost $5,000.

Using State Activities

States are either active or inactive. A state becomes *active* when its entry activity is executed. A state becomes *inactive* after its exit activity is executed. (You can see examples of entry and exit activities in Figure 7-3.) A good demonstration of an implementation of entry and exit activities can be seen in events written for when a control gains focus and loses focus. For example, when we open a refrigerator door, a light is turned on, and when we close the door, the light is turned off.

States can contain additional activities. These are divided into categories: regular and do. A *regular activity* is something that happens instantaneously. An activity prefixed with "do/" is called a *do activity*. Do activities happen over time. For example,

a regular activity might be complete in a few uninterruptible machine instructions or perhaps could be longer if it occurred within a thread critical section. A do activity happens over many instructions and can be interrupted by an event, for example.

Consider the Visual SourceSafe application in Figure 7-4. If you click a high-level node and choose the "Get Latest Version" option, then you could be waiting a while because copying hundreds or thousands of files from a source code repository across a network to a workstation is time-consuming. Conscientiously, such a long-running operation should be interruptible. Using a simple do activity in a state indicates that this is an intended part of design.

Comparing Simple and Composite States

A *simple state* is a state with no substructure. Having no substructure means that the state is not divided into regions, and there are no substates. A *composite state* (also called a *superstate*) has an internal structure that may include regions and does include substates. The "Door Closed" state in Figure 7-3 is a composite state. It is also a *nonorthogonal* state.

A *nonorthogonal* composite state means that there are nested substates, and only one is active at a time. For example, in Figure 7-3, only "Heating" or "Off" is active at one time. An orthogonal composite state is a state divided into concurrently executing regions. Only one substate in each region is active at a time.

Figure 7-3 is an example of a nonorthogonal composite state. To create an orthogonal composite state, split the state symbol into regions, and place substates into their respective regions. Figure 7-5 shows an orthogonal composite state representing a refrigerator freezer. Cooling and freezing happen concurrently in separate compartments, but lighting happens when either door is opened.

Tip *Visio doesn't do a great job of managing composite states. Visio supports composite substates by adding a linked child state chart when you add a composite state to a diagram. Advanced features such as composite orthogonal substates are supported in more advanced (and more expensive) tools. Such tools may be worth the price of admission if you are frequently using advanced features not found in tools such as Visio.*

Figure 7-4   A state with a "do/activity Getting Latest Version"; the "do/" means that this state can be interrupted.

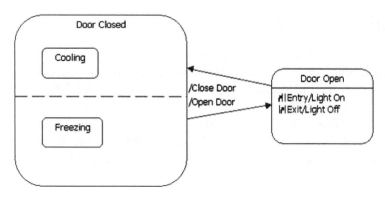

Figure 7-5   A composite orthogonal state that represents simultaneous cooling and freezing.

Figure 7-3 was laboriously created using MS-Paint, whereas Figure 7-5 was created much more quickly using Rational XDE. I do a lot of modeling, so it is worth the price of admission to use Rational XDE, but on some projects, I have used Visio, and it works fine for day-to-day modeling. Good tools are the mark of a good craftsperson, but spending a lot of money is no guarantee of success.

Using Internal Activities

Internal activities are like self-transitions—refer to "Exploring Transitions" below. An *internal activity* is a response that happens internally and triggers an activity without executing an exit and entry activity. Internal activities use the same event, guard, and activity notation that is used on transitions. I'll talk more about transitions shortly.

Linking to Submachines

Instead of repeating state chart (state machine) diagrams, you want to reuse diagrams. This applies to state machines. The UML supports modeling submachines by naming the substate machine after the state name, separated by a class name. (This looks like the C++ variable-class name declaration statement.) For example,

```
mystate : MyStateMachine
```

indicates that "MyState" is an instance of the state machine named "MyState-Machine."

If you are using Visio, then you can use the name, colon, state machine notation to reference a substate machine. Other tools—such as Rational XDE, mentioned previously—support a special symbol for submachines and will link the referenced submachine dynamically.

Exploring Transitions

Transitions are directed lines that connect states. Transitions occur based on some triggering mechanism—commonly implemented as events—and may or may not proceed based on a guard condition, resulting in some effect. This sort of cause-and-effect relationship illustrates why state machines can be useful for modeling user interfaces. This section will explore triggering mechanisms, examples of guard conditions, and how to specify effects. I also will complete the discussion of internal and external transitions introduced in the section "Using Internal Activities."

Specifying Triggers

A transition has a source state, a transition event, a guard, an effect, and a target state. Before the source state is exited, the exit activity occurs. When the transition trigger occurs, a guard condition can be tested to determine if the transition is taken. A taken transition results in an effect. Finally, the target's entry activity is executed. The directed line that represents the transition is labeled with the optional trigger event, guard, and effect. If the activities in a state finish, then the result is called a *triggerless* or *completion transition.*

Triggers, or events, that signify a transition are categorized as *call, change, signal*, and *timer events.* A call event specifies a synchronous object call. A change event represents a change in the result of a Boolean expression. A signal event indicates an explicit, named synchronous message, and a timer event is a trigger that occurs after a specific interval of time. The trigger is the first element, if present, attached to a transition.

TIP *Some tools may prefix specific kinds of transitions with labels such as "when" in the case of Visio and change events.*

Specifying Guard Conditions

Guard conditions are placed in brackets and must evaluate to a testable Boolean condition. (I have seen the notation for guard conditions on other diagrams, such as activity and interaction diagrams.) If a guard condition is present, then it is evaluated and must result in a true value for the transition to complete.

Guard conditions should be relatively simple and should not result in side effects. For example, "[x > 0]" is a good guard condition, but "increment x during the evaluation like [x++ > 0]" is a guard with side effects because the value of x is changed each time the guard is executed.

NOTE *Formal modeling evolved after formal coding practices. Many good practices, such as not writing conditional code with side effects, mirror practices desirable in code, and generally, models end up as code.*

Specifying Effects

Triggers, guards, and effects are all optional. The last element of a transition symbol is the option effect (or activity). The effect is some activity that is to be performed when the transition is triggered. The signature of a transition, including a trigger, guard, and effect, is

```
Event[Guard]/Effect
```

You also might see events referred to as *triggers* and effects referred to as *activities.* Although a lot of synonyms can be confusing, these words are close enough to convey their purpose.

According to the formal specification, there may be many triggers, one guard, and one activity. Supporting zero to many triggers means that more than one event may result in a transition. Supporting a single guard does not mean that the guard cannot have multiple predicates (subexpressions that yield a Boolean result), and a single effect does not mean that the effect cannot be a compound effect. (In addition, the target state can perform many activities too.) Figure 7-6 shows several transitions with some or all of the elements described in this section.

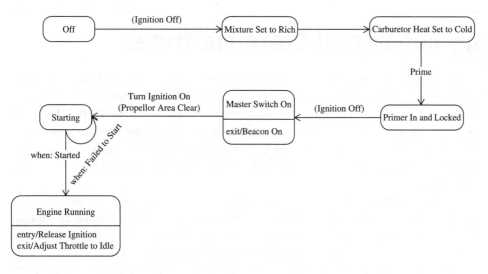

Figure 7-6 A variety of transitions showing optional transition elements.

In the figure, we are showing a state machine that reflects the state of a single-engine aircraft between the off and idling states. The state machine models the engine as a complex system with a progression of transitions and states, with the final state being that the engine is running and idling.

NOTE *In a digital system, it is easy to enforce such things as "the ignition must be off before the master switch is turned on," but in an analog system, we could easily turn a propeller into a human Cuisinart. As modelers, our job is to capture the rules; sometimes rules cannot be enforced, especially in analog systems.*

Reviewing Transition Kinds

I talked about several kinds of transitions. Let me take a moment to review those here.

An entry transition occurs when a state is first entered before anything else in the state happens. An exit transition is the last thing to happen before a state exits. An external transition can be a self-transition or a transition to another state. A self-transition occurs when a state exits and reenters itself. A self-transition is shown in Figure 7-6 when the "Starting" state fails and we return to the "Starting" state for an additional attempt. Finally, an internal transition is a response to an event that doesn't result in a change of state. Internal transitions do not cause an exit and entry activity to be executed.

Creating Behavioral State Machines

Behavior state machines are intended to model precise behavior and are implemented as code. Consequently, behavioral state machines use most of the elements available for creating state charts (or state machine diagrams). The UML version 2.0 precisely defines elements that are intended for protocol state machines and those intended for behavioral state machines. However, if you need an element in a behavioral state machine, then use it, even if it isn't specifically intended for a behavioral state machine.

Figure 7-7 puts many of the elements together and describes a behavioral state machine. This machine begins with a motorcycle in the stopped state and transitions to prestart and running states, including a path for returning to the stopped state. (The text in italics labels various elements of the diagram.)

A key to diagramming a behavioral state machine is to determine how much information to put in your model. The model in Figure 7-7 might describe enough

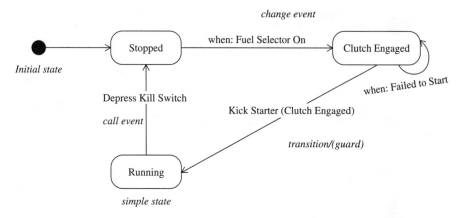

Figure 7-7   A behavioral state machine that cycles through stopped and running states on my motorcycle.

information for a rider starting a motorcycle, but if we needed to understand how the fuel, transmission, and ignition systems worked too, then this diagram would be insufficient. As with programming, the caveat "*Divid et impera*" applies here too. What I mean by divide and conquer is that we probably would model the various subsystems—ignition, fuel, and transmission—separately and use substate machine references to incorporate those elements into the diagram in Figure 7-7. The premise is that our diagram is a good starting point, but adding too many elements, resulting in a single monolithic diagram, is probably more complexity than can be grasped at a glance. Complex diagrams counteract the value of modeling.

Creating Protocol State Machines

Protocol state machines have to do with defining a series of predictable, logical sequences. Protocol state machines are not meant to be implemented, but they are meant to describe the order of transitions and states. For this reason, protocol state machines are used to describe interfaces. Because interfaces don't have definitions, many of the elements you use in behavioral state machines just aren't needed in protocol state machines.

Consider the ordered use of a database. We can say that a database connection is created, the connection is opened, data are retrieved, and the connection is closed. This describes a protocol that can be implemented as an interface (or interfaces) for a predictable and reliable logical sequence of steps—a protocol—for ensuring that

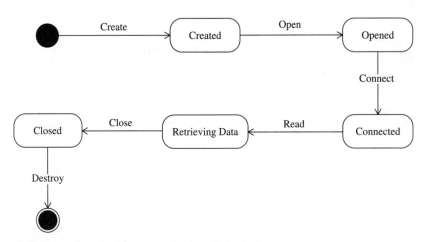

Figure 7-8 A protocol state machine that shows the logical, reliable sequence of events that has to occur to use a database connection correctly every time.

a connection is used correctly every time. Figure 7-8 shows the protocol state machine described here.

A protocol state machine can be used to show developers at a high level how to use parts of the system correctly every time. By defining an interface with these elements, you would provide them with a means of following the protocol. The state machine shown in Figure 7-8 could be used as a training aid to ensure that a valuable resource such as a database connection is not used incorrectly.

Implementing State Diagrams

Activity diagrams show how a single use case is supported. Interaction diagrams show the time ordering of object creation and sent messages but are not good at showing how objects are implemented. State machines show an object as it spans several use cases and are designed to show how objects should be implemented. Perhaps one of the reasons state machines seem to be used less often than interaction diagrams is because state machines are closer to code than other kinds of diagrams, and the closer we get to code, the more tempted programmers are to start coding.

In high-ceremony software development, there may be a mandate that dictates the number and variety of diagrams to create. (I have worked on a couple, but they are rare.) Because state machines are close to lines of code, I would only create state machines for risky, complicated, or rare kinds of subsystems. GUI prototyping works great for most applications and has an appeasing effect on users. State machines representing GUIs do not seem to satisfy the need for tangible evidence of progress, as well as interactive, visually stimulating prototypes.

This said, Fowler (2000) states that a state machine can be implemented in one of three ways: nested switch, the state behavior pattern, and state tables. A *nested switch statement* is exactly what it sounds like: Some semantic constant value is evaluated, and a series of if..conditionals, select, case, or switch statements determines which branch block of code to execute. Using a nested switch is the least object-oriented way of implementing a state machine. The second listed choice is the state pattern. The *state pattern* defines abstract behaviors, and the state machine is implemented by calling specific instances of subclasses of the abstract state class. This is a powerful object-oriented way of implementing stateful behavior. Finally, we can use external state tables. A *state table* stores the source, trigger, guard, effect, and target information in a database, XML file, or something similar. While this isn't an object-oriented approach, it is the most flexible approach because we can change the state table without modifying, rebuilding, and redeploying code.

The following listing shows how we might implement the microwave oven's (from Figure 7-3) behavior using a switch statement. While this code is functional, it can be the most difficult to implement, read, and maintain.

```
using System;
namespace MicrowaveOven
{
  public enum DoorState{ Closed, Opened };
  public enum LightState{ Off, On };
  public enum MicrowaveEmitterState{ Off, On };
  public enum TimerState{ Off, Paused, On };

  class Class1
  {
    private DoorState door;
    private LightState light;
    private MicrowaveEmitterState emitter;
    private TimerState timer;

    [STAThread]
    static void Main(string[] args)
    {
    }

    public DoorState Door
    {
      get{ return door; }
      set{ door = value; }
    }

    public LightState Light
    {
      get{ return light; }
      set{ light = value; }
```

```
    }

    public MicrowaveEmitterState Emitter
    {
      get{ return emitter; }
      set{ emitter = value; }
    }

    public TimerState Timer
    {
      get{ return timer; }
      set{ timer = value; }
    }

    public void OpenDoor()
    {
      ChangeDoorState(DoorState.Opened);
    }

    public void CloseDoor()
    {
      ChangeDoorState(DoorState.Closed);
    }

    private void ChangeDoorState(DoorState doorState)
    {
      switch(doorState)
      {
        case DoorState.Closed:
          door = DoorState.Closed;
          switch(timer)
          {
            case TimerState.Off:
              light = LightState.Off;
              break;
            case TimerState.Paused:
              timer = TimerState.On;
              emitter = MicrowaveEmitterState.On;
              light = LightState.On;
              break;
            case TimerState.On:
              throw new Exception("your brain is being poached");
          }
          break;

        case DoorState.Opened:
          switch(timer)
          {
            case TimerState.Off:
              break;
            case TimerState.On:
              emitter = MicrowaveEmitterState.Off;
              timer = TimerState.Paused;
              break;
            case TimerState.Paused:
```

```
            break;
        }
        light = LightState.On;
        door = DoorState.Opened;
        break;
    }
  }
 }
}
```

We could implement the rules in a table and read the table for each transition (Table 7-1). Although we would be unlikely to change the microwave states after deployment, this approach is used commonly in Web application portals such as dotnetnuke or IBUYSPY.

The prior code listing works pretty well because we can easily codify the nested relationships reflecting the substates of "Heating" and "Off." Table 7-1 isn't completely satisfactory because we have to surface the nested substates to capture desired behaviors when the door is closed and we resume nuking the food. (The meaning is pretty clear in the table; we could add an additional column to clearly indicate substates.) For an example of the state behavior pattern, see Chapter 9.

It is worth noting that the state pattern, a switch, or an external table won't implement an entire state machine. These three options represent a general approach, but basic code and other patterns are useful here too. For example, we can use the Memento behavior pattern to facilitate capturing and restoring an object's internal state. For more information on patterns, see Chapter 9, and pick up a copy of *Design Patterns*, by Erich Gamma et al.

Source	Trigger	Guard	Effect	Target
Door Closed	Open Door		Light On	Door Opened
Door Opened	Close Door		Light Off	Door Closed
Heating	Open Door		Light On, Emitter Off, Timer Paused	Door Opened
Off	Open Door		Light On	Door Opened
Door Opened	Close Door		Light On, Emitter On, Timer On	Heating
Door Opened	Close Door		Light Off	Off

Table 7-1   This Table Could Be Externalized in a Database or XML File, Permitting Behaviors to Be Changed Post-Deployment

Quiz

1. State charts (or state machine diagrams) are good for

   a. diagramming systems.

   b. diagramming objects and messages for a single use case.

   c. understanding a single use case.

   d. specifying the behavior of an object across several use cases.

2. State machines are especially useful in exploring GUIs and real-time controllers.

   a. True

   b. False

3. A junction is used to

   a. merge several incoming transitions to a single outgoing transition.

   b. split a single incoming transition into several outgoing transitions.

   c. Both a and b

   d. None of the above

4. History pseudostates are used to restore previous states.

   a. True

   b. False

5. A regular activity executes

   a. over time and a do activity executes immediately but can be interrupted.

   b. immediately and a do activity executes over time and can be interrupted.

   c. over time and can be interrupted and a do activity executes over time.

   d. over time and a do activity executes overtime; only the do activity can be interrupted.

6. Transitions are directed lines labeled with

   a. an optional trigger event, a guard, and an effect.

   b. a trigger event, an optional guard, and an effect.

   c. a trigger event, a guard, and an optional effect.

   d. optionally, a trigger event, a guard, and an effect.

7. Internal transitions cause an enter and exit activity to be executed.

   a. True

   b. False

8. Self-transitions cause an enter and exit activity to be executed.

   a. True

   b. False

9. A composite orthogonal state

   a. is divided into regions, and only one region can be active at a time.

   b. is divided into regions, and only one substate can be active at a time.

   c. is divided into regions, and only one substate per region can be active at a time.

   d. is composed of a single region, and multiple substates can be active simultaneously.

10. A composite nonorthogonal state

   a. is composed of regions, and only one region can be active at a time.

   b. is not divided into regions, and only one substate can be active at a time.

   c. is not divided into regions, and multiple substates can be active at a time.

   d. is divided into regions, and one substate per region can be active at a time.

Answers

1. d

2. a

3. c

4. a

5. b

6. a

7. b

8. a

9. c

10. b

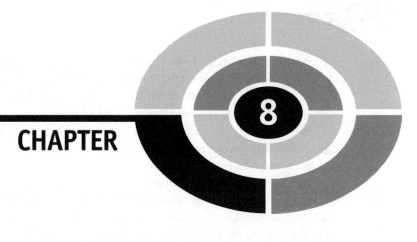

CHAPTER

8

Modeling Components

When I was 15, I purchased my first car for $325. Go ahead and laugh—a $325 car in 1981 was as bad as you'd imagine it to be. Of course, being industrious, I began to find ways to refurbish the car and make it as roadworthy as I knew how. One of the first things I realized about this 1974 Oldsmobile Cutlass rust bucket—besides that the front seat didn't lock, causing the seat to slide all the way forward when I stopped and all the way back when I accelerated, the football-sized hole in the radiator, and four different sized tires—was that the serpentine belt needed replacing. I thought replacing a serpentine belt was a task I could handle.

After I got the car home, I settled on replacing the serpentine belt. I began to remove the radiator, water pump, and alternator. You get the picture. I realized that this was a bigger job than I might be able to do and resolved to take the car to the

Firestone repair shop down the road. The Firestone guy loosened the alternator, rotating it inward, slipped the belt over the fan and alternator, moved the alternator back into place, tightened the bolts, and was finished in 10 minutes. I just received my first $35 dollar lesson in the value of knowledge.

Why did I tell you this story? The answer is because when I tell you that you can probably skim over this chapter and may not need component diagrams, you will believe me.

To model components, we use many of the same symbols and connectors that we have discussed in earlier chapters, but there is a difference. *Components* are autonomous chunks of code—think subsystem—that can be reused by deploying them independently. (Components don't have to be big, but they generally are much more than a single class or a couple of loosely related classes.) Components generally have multiple provided and required interfaces and are found in large, complex applications with dozens or hundreds of domain classes. Thus, if you are building a simple client-server application, a basic Web site, or single-user Windows application, then you probably don't need component diagrams. If you are building an enterprise solution with hundreds of domain classes and reusable elements, then you might need component diagrams.

Every class is not a domain class. Arrays, collections, and graphical user interface (GUI) classes are not domain classes. Domain classes are the things that capture the domain problem—student, registration, classes in an enrollment application, bookings, people, cases, time served in a prison management application, and deposits, withdrawals, and accounts in a banking system. If you have hundreds of these kinds of classes, then you may need component diagrams.

Obvious examples of very complex components include such things as Microsoft Office applications, Enterprise Java Beans, COM+, and CORBA. Perhaps less complex components might include your custom database persistence component.

This said, I encourage you to just skim this chapter, but you should read it thoroughly if you know you are building a big system or are trying to organize the efforts of a large team and an overview of the system will help orchestrate the efforts of all the developers. This chapter will show the straightforward mechanics of creating component diagrams. For excellent guidelines on the circumstances for building component diagrams, refer to Scott Ambler's *The Object Primer: Agile Model-Driven Development with UML 2.0,* 3rd edition. In this chapter you will learn

- How to describe components
- How to specify provided and required interfaces
- Alternate ways to specify a component based on the detail you want to convey

Introducing Component-Based Design

There are two general ways to derive components. One way is to use a top-down approach, and another way is to use a bottom-up approach. Either way can work. Let me explain what I mean by both approaches and why either way can work.

Using a Top-Down Approach to Design

A top-down approach is a recommended approach by some. What a top-down approach means is that you define the components first—the big pieces of the system—and then define the component interfaces. Once the components and interfaces are defined, you can divide the implementation of the system among the participants by having various groups or team members build each component. Since everyone theoretically has agreed to build to the interfaces, the developers are free to implement the internal parts of the component any way they choose.

I think that this approach can work if your team is using many well-established components with well-known interfaces. However, defining all new components from a top-down perspective can be very challenging to do well and to get right.

Additionally, using a top-down approach means that you are committing to a complex implementation style from the get-go because component-based systems have as many as three to five supporting interfaces and pass-through classes for every domain class. (This is what components are—discrete, well-defined interfaces resulting in indirection and pass-through classes.)

Thus the problem with a top-down approach is that for every domain class you might design (and implement), you need five support classes, and this is why component-based systems can be time-consuming, expensive, and risky.

Using a Bottom-Up Approach to Design

A bottom-up approach means that you define domain classes first—i.e., the classes that solve the business problem, not the architectural problem. The result is that a significant amount of effort is spent on solving the problem first rather than designing a complicated architecture first.

With domain classes and a bottom-up approach, you get more traction on solving the problem, and you always can componentize the domain classes if the complexity of your solution grows or you identify a group of classes that can be deployed and reused more easily if they are encapsulated in components.

Either a top-down or a bottom-up approach can work. For small to medium-sized applications, you probably don't need many components, and a bottom-up design will work fine. For enterprise-scale applications, you need an experienced guide, and a top-down approach may be best.

A critical concept is that decisions are easier to change in models than they are in code. Thus, if you do create models, you can explore and change design decisions more readily. This concept applies to component diagrams too.

Modeling a Component

In the Unified Modeling Language (UML), the component symbol was changed from the unwieldy symbol shown in Figure 8-1 to a classifier symbol—a rectangle—with the «component» stereotype (Figure 8-2) or a small icon that looks like Figure 8-1 in the upper-right corner of the classifier symbol.

We have to compromise with some UML tools that aren't completely compatible with UML version 2.0. The classifier in Figure 8-2 shows the attribute and operation sections of the classifier symbol. This is acceptable.

If your tool supports the old-style symbol (shown in Figure 8-1), then you can use that as well. Apparently, the reason for the symbol change was that the older-style symbol's jutting rectangles made it more difficult to draw and attach connectors.

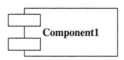

Figure 8-1   The old-style UML component symbol.

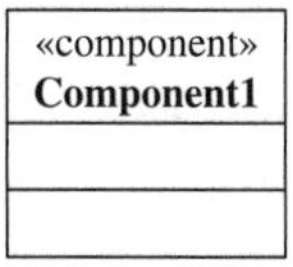

«component»
Component1

Figure 8-2   The revised component symbol in UML version 2.0.

Specifying Provided and Required Interfaces

In Chapter 6 we introduced provided and required interfaces. A *provided interface* is represented by the lollipop extending from the interface, and a *required interface* is represented by the half lollipop extending from the interface. In simple terms, a provided interface is an interface the component defines, and a required interface is one that it needs to be complete. Figure 8-3 illustrates part of a financial system that shows the account management component and the persistence (database, typically) layer.

Don't get hung up on the limitations of your modeling tool. More than likely, if your tool generates code, then it will generate it based on the correct use of symbols for the subset of the version of UML that your tool supports. For example, in Figure 8-3 we see the jutting smaller rectangles, and we had to fabricate the ball-and-socket look for required and provided interfaces, which for this version of UML actually works to defeat the tool.

If your tool has the same limitation as Visio 2003—which doesn't support the half lollipop—then you could indicate provided and required interface relationships using the dependency connector (Figure 8-4).

***

Note   *The half-lollipop and full-lollipop connectors and classifiers are metaphorically referred to as a* wiring diagram. *If you've ever seen a wiring diagram, then you might see the similarities.*

Figure 8-3   The "AccountManager" component provides the "Account" interface and requires the "Persistence" interface.

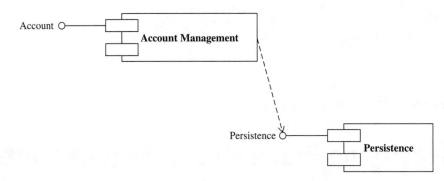

Figure 8-4   Using a dependency in place of the half lollipop to model a required interface when UML version 2.0 isn't completely supported by your modeling tool.

Exploring Component Modeling Styles

There are different ways to diagram the same component based on the information we want to show. If a diagram is for an implementer, then you may want to show a whitebox—internal details shown—diagram of a component. If the diagram is for a consumer, then you only need to show the provided and required interfaces. If you want to show the implementation of provided interfaces, then you can use a classifier and dependencies—because classifiers are better at showing implementation details of interfaces.

In this section we will look at some variations on component diagrams, including diagrams with more elements. (For this section of the chapter I switched to Poseidon for UML version 3.1. Poseidon for UML version 3.1 has better support for UML version 2.0 component diagrams than either of the copies of Rational XDE or Visio. When modeling an actual application or system, I encourage you to use one tool and to use the notation that is most readily available. However, in a book format, switching tools gives you an idea of some of the variety out there.)

Diagramming Components for Consumers

When you are creating component diagrams for consumers—other programmers who will use the components—all you need to show them is a blackbox view of the component. A blackbox view of a component provides the details of the provided and required interfaces. If your tool supports it, you can use a component symbol and list the provided and required interfaces, including the method signatures exposed, or you can show classifiers stereotyped with «interface». Most tools support the realizations, dependencies, and classifiers, so the latter style is easier to create.

A provided interface represents an interface that the component realizes; thus, when using classifiers, the lollipop becomes the realization connector. A required interface represents an interface in which the component depends; thus, when using classifiers, the half lollipop becomes the dependency connector with a «use» stereotype. Figure 8-5 is a blackbox diagram showing the provided interfaces "IExceptionXMLPublisher" and "IExceptionPublisher" and the required interface "IConfigSectionHandler." (This is a partial component diagram of the Exception Management Application Block for .NET offered by Microsoft and used in Motownjobs.com.)

In Figure 8-5, the reader knows that the "ExceptionManagement" component realizes "IExceptionXMLPublisher" and "IExceptionPublisher," which are elements that the consumer will be able to use. The reader also knows that something called "IConfigSectionHandler" is something that the component needs.

NOTE *If you are interested in .NET and application blocks, then you can obtain more information at* www.microsoft.com. *Application blocks basically are components that solve reusable problems at a higher level of abstraction than simply classes in a framework.*

If the context is unknown, then this diagram doesn't provide enough information, but once we place the component in a context—in this case, in the .NET framework—the datatypes and the required interfaces become available to the consumer.

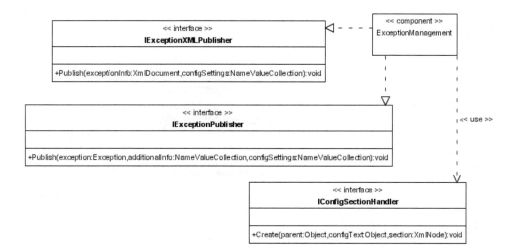

Figure 8-5 Provided and required interfaces modeled using realization and dependency connectors and classifiers to elaborate on the definition.

Diagramming Components for Producers

If we are diagramming components for producers—those who will implement the component—then we need more information. For producers, we need to show internal components, classes, and relationships that the component implementer will have to create as code. This is what I am referring to as a whitebox, or internal details, view.

We can elaborate on the component diagram in Figure 8-5 and add internal details about the "ExceptionManagement" component. Figure 8-6 shows the provided and required interfaces as lollipops and expands the focus on internal elements of the component.

Figure 8-6 shows the same provided and required interfaces, but our internal whitebox view now shows how we support some of the external elements. Although this view still may not provide every detail needed to implement the "Exception-Management" component, we could add attributes and operations to classifiers and combine the component diagram with other diagrams such as state charts, class diagrams, and sequences. Collectively, the various diagrams would explain how to implement the component.

It is worth noting that we are expressing the same kinds of relationships we have seen before in class diagrams. It is also worth noting that components, like classes, can contain nested elements such as nested components.

To experiment with component modeling, find a domain that you are familiar with or an existing solution, such as the Northwind sample database. See if you can

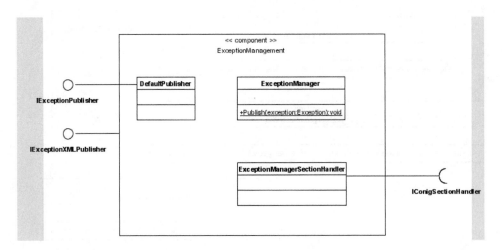

Figure 8-6   This figure switches focus to emphasize the internal, or whitebox, view of the component.

describe a top-down view of a "componentized" version of elements of a customer order-fulfillment system. (Of course, you can use any sample domain with which you are familiar.)

Quiz

1. Every model should contain at least one component diagram.

    a. True

    b. False

2. A top-down approach to component diagrams means that you

    a. define the components first and then decompose those components into constituent parts.

    b. define the constituent parts and then place the components on top of the constituent parts.

    c. None of the above

3. A bottom-up approach to design can be valuable because (pick all that apply)

    a. components aren't really needed.

    b. you get more traction solving domain problems first.

    c. building infrastructure is expensive and time-consuming.

    d. domain classes always can be organized into components at a later time.

4. Component symbols can be represented using a classifier with the «component» stereotype.

    a. True

    b. False

5. A provided interface can be represented by a named lollipop

    a. or a half lollipop.

    b. or a dependency on a classifier with the «interface» stereotype.

    c. or an «interface» stereotype on a classifier with a realization connector.

    d. only by using the lollipop.

6. A required interface is an interface that the component realizes.

    a. True

    b. False

7. A required interface can be represented by a named half lollipop

   a. or a lollipop.

   b. or a dependency on a classifier with the «interface» stereotype.

   c. or an «interface» stereotype on a classifier with a realization connector.

   d. only by using the half lollipop.

8. Components can contain nested components.

   a. True

   b. False

9. As a general rule, you only components and component diagrams for systems with 100 or more domain classes.

   a. True, but this is a general guideline. Components can help you to organize a solution and build reusable elements that can be sold separately.

   b. False, because building components is always cheaper in the long run.

10. For each domain class in a component-based architecture, you may need three to five supporting classes.

    a. True

    b. False

Answers

1. b
2. a
3. b, c, and d
4. a
5. c
6. b
7. b
8. a
9. a
10. a

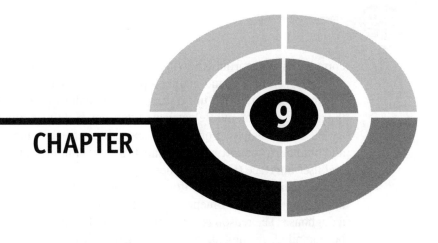

Fit and Finish

I have worked on projects with budgets of less than $5 million that encompassed 20,000 person-hours to projects with budgets of over a billion dollars and hundreds of thousands of person-hours. Some of these projects used almost no formal modeling and design, and others used so much modeling and design that all forward momentum came to a halt. The lesson is that too little formality can result in a hacky, shoddy product and too much formality can result in a stalled or canceled project.

It is also worth mentioning that I have worked for huge companies that don't do any modeling but deliver software all the time. One has to wonder if the success of those projects is related to how much money those companies had to throw at the problem and also whether the software would be better, faster, and cheaper if some modeling and design had occurred.

The answer is somewhere in between. In general, software models need to be as complete and precise as the thing being designed. For example, if you are building something as complex as a doghouse, then you probably don't need much in the way of models. For something as complex as a house, you probably need models as complex as a blueprint. Knowing the size, number of rooms, and building materials will help you to size and budget a project while leaving some room for invention. For instance, variations in lighting fixtures, color of paint, style of carpeting, and the precise placement of electrical outlets can be left (within reason) to the ingenuity of the specialists. For houses, specialists are carpenters, electricians, roofers, and plumbers; for software, specialists are programmers, testers, DBAs, and graphical user interface (GUI) designers.

The reality is that most software is more complex than a house, and much of it is being built without blueprints (UML models) that would adequately describe a doghouse. The reason is that software modeling is new and hard. Further, code can be compiled, debugged, run, and tested with results that are superficially measurable. In contrast, models aren't compiled but can only be "debugged" manually, are not run, and there is no simple way to test them. I would wager that very few software companies are doing code walk-throughs successfully, forget about Unified Modeling Language (UML) walkthroughs.

What all this means is that if you are reading this, then you are ahead of many of your peers in terms of software modeling practices. It also means that defining a process and finding a balance between too much and too little modeling are important. In this chapter I have provided some practical pointers in the context of UML modeling and design that have helped me in the past. These pointers are based on some projects that have succeeded and some that have failed. To help you figure out how to complete your models, I will talk about

- A few basic dos and don'ts
- Using known patterns and refactorings
- When and how to add supporting documentation
- Validating your models

Modeling Dos and Don'ts

I thought about naming this section "Modeling Best Practices" but dos and don'ts seems more demystifying.

I started modeling using the Booch notation in the early 1990s. In those days, there were few places you could go to learn a language such as C++ from a seasoned pro and almost nowhere to learn modeling. This means that early on, the few books I could get and my own mistakes were the only teachers available. Over more than a dozen years, I have gotten better, but there are still few bona fide modeling experts, and as far as I can tell, many universities still aren't offering curricula for software architects (or even UML modelers); the art is too new. Consequently, the advice I can give you is based on my own intensive study and many years of feeling my way. Clearly, this all suggests that your local expert may disagree with my opinion. You know your own people better than I do; if you think that something won't work or that my advice is questionable, then look to those few wise old men whom everybody recognizes as experts: James Rumbaugh, Ivar Jacobson, Grady Booch, Erich Gamma, and Martin Fowler. There are a few others, but you get the picture. When I have questions about the UML modeling, these are the folks I turn too.

Don't Keep Programmers Waiting

The first rule is: *Don't keep programmers waiting on models.* This means that you must do a lot of design before you assemble your main programming team. A few programmers available to help you prototype will be helpful, but don't staff up completely until you have a project plan and some of the analysis and design well under way.

Unfortunately, most projects aren't this organized. The whole team arrives, and the pressure is on immediately to get everyone to work, including programmers. Try to create models that are detailed enough to get programmers working but not so detailed that they are stuck waiting. This is hard to do.

Work from a Macro View to a Micro View

Work on "big picture" items first. For example, identify the big parts of the system first—Web GUI, custom macro language, Web services, and database persistence—before working on classes and lines of code. If you can figure out the parts and how they fit together, then work can be divided by subsystems. This is a top-down approach, but it supports a division of labor and gives you a context for smaller, more detailed work.

Document Sparingly

Most documentation is part of the micro view. When modeling, keep in mind that the UML is a shorthand language for text. (You could design a whole system in plain English, right?) Analyze and design a solution as completely as needed without adding a lot of notes and documentation. Often, additional diagrams can clarify a diagram as readily as long-winded text.

You also can save some of the documentation for the end of the project if your models are hard deliverables. If your customer (internal or external) isn't paying for the models, then spending resources polishing them may be a waste of your time and money.

Find an Editor

Being a good UML modeler is not the same as being a good writer. In addition to getting a second set of eyes to look at your UML diagrams, hire an English major (or whatever language you speak) to review your documentation. Again, only do this if models are hard deliverables.

Be Selective about Diagrams You Choose to Create

Why did the chicken cross the road? The answer is probably because she could. Don't create diagrams because you can. Only create those that solve interesting problems and only those that you really need. This approach also will help to eliminate the waiting programmer problem.

Don't Count on Code Generation

James McCarthy cautions against "flipping the bozo bit"—as in "that guy is a bozo"— but if someone tells you that you are to model, model, model and flip a switch generating an executable, then *flip that bozo bit*. We are a decade or two away from the technology and education supporting generated applications. I have never seen this approach work and have talked to several Rational consultants who agree with me. Code generation is a good idea, but we are a long way from automating software generation.

Model and Build from Most Risky to Least Risky

Software usually has a few very important business cases and a bunch of supporting business cases. The guiding principle is to build the hardest and most important parts of the software first. Tackling the hard problems first helps you to avoid nasty surprises, and frequently, software can ship if the important business cases are supported even when some of the extra frills aren't so great. In my experience, this is one of the biggest mistakes projects make: building easy things first.

If It's Obvious Don't Model It

Application blocks, components, third-party tools, and frameworks are all out of your control. All you can do is use them—unless you own these elements too, which is rare. Don't waste time modeling what you don't own. If you must model third-party tools in order to help developers use them, then model them as black-boxes: All you need to model is their presence and interfaces, and you only need to model the interfaces you are actually using. If your developers can use ADO.NET or the Data Access Application Block, for example, then simply indicate that you are using it. That's enough.

Emphasize Specialization

Another mistake is team member generalization. Software teams consist of gener-alists, but there is a tremendous amount of historical documentation and evidence that specialization is a good thing: Adam Smith's *Wealth of Nations*, Henry Ford's assembly lines, and the ancient Latin phrase "*Divid et imperum.*" Dividing a prob-lem, intensity of focus, specialization, and building the critical elements first will take you a long way on the road to success.

Using Known State Patterns

Patterns are not an original idea or new. The application of patterns in software seems to originate from a 1977 book entitled, *A Pattern Language*, by Christopher Alexander et al. Oddly enough, this book is about designing cities and towns, and patterns such as *green spaces*. The green space pattern means that towns should have parks.

It is certainly a clever extrapolation to turn a book about designing cities into a concept that revolutionizes software—does it happen any other way than by ex-trapolation—but it has been demonstrated that good pattern usage helps to yield good software. The question is: Since software patterns are documented, do you need to add them to your UML diagrams when you use them in your designs? The answer is probably.

Software patterns are templates, but there is some latitude in how you implement them. Each time a pattern is employed, you will have different class names based on the solution domain, and many patterns can be implemented in different ways. For example, events and event handlers are an implementation of the observer pattern, but this is not precisely how observer is documented. Microsoft considers ASP pages and code-behind for ASP.NET an implementation of model-view-controller (MVC), but you won't see ASP.NET mentioned in the pattern definition. Thus the answer is yes, in many instances, if you use a pattern, then you should incorporate it into your models to place it in the context of your problem domain. However, if you have a very experienced team, then you could just tell the developers to use the MVC, observer, or state pattern here.

TIP *A good tip is to identify patterns when you use them. Identifying well-documented design patterns will eliminate or at least mitigate the need for you to duplicate that documentation in your designs.*

A good rule of thumb is that good software is based on patterns. The key is to learn about design patterns, figure out key areas where they will help your design, and then incorporate them into your designs.

Figure 9-1 demonstrates how we can model the state behavior pattern, borrowing from the microwave oven in Chapter 7. This example demonstrates how we can

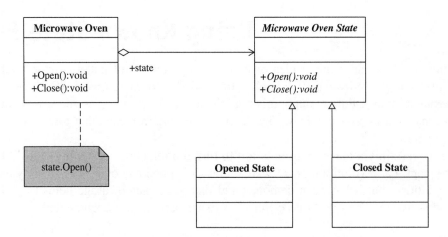

Figure 9-1 This figure is a classic implementation of the state behavior pattern for the microwave oven example from Chapter 7.

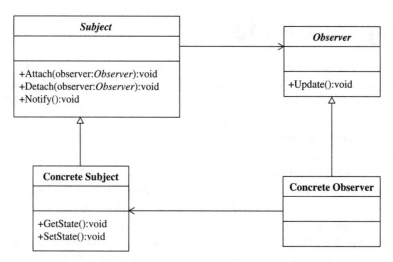

Figure 9-2   A classic diagram of the observer pattern, also known as *publish-subscribe*.

model a known pattern where only the names change. Figure 9-2 shows the classic model of the observer pattern, and Figure 9-3 shows a variation of the observer pattern reflecting variations in the classic model but observer nonetheless.

Notice that in the classic example of observer (see Figure 9-2) an interface is not used. However, in Figure 9-3 I used an interface. The result is that anything can implement "IListener" and play the role of listener. This implementation is useful in singly inheriting languages and is useful for moving messages around an application in a unified way. The reason for adding this model and indicating that it is an implementation of observer is that it is different from the classic implementation, but the documentation for observer still helps to clarify the rationale for its use.

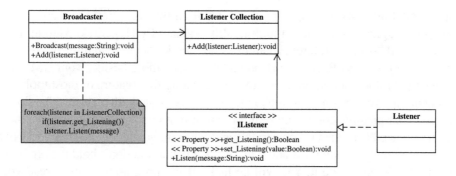

Figure 9-3   A variation of the observer behavior pattern that I refer to as *broadcast-listen*, which is very close to the publish-subscribe notion of observer.

Refactoring Your Model

This book is not the best forum for teaching design patterns or refactoring. The UML is distinct from patterns, but patterns are described using the UML and text in other books. Refactoring is different from both the UML and patterns. While there is some overlap between patterns and refactorings—e.g., Singleton and Factory are both creational patterns and refactorings—refactoring is something that generally is done after code has been written to improve the design of existing code. This said, there is no reason you cannot refactor models.

Suppose, for example, that you have a message signature in an interaction diagram that has several parameters. Before you release the diagram to your programmers, you could apply the refactoring "Introduce Parameter Object." "Introduce Parameter Object" simply says to convert a long method signature into a short method signature by introducing a class that contains all the parameters needed for a particular method and changing the method to accept an instance of that class.

There is no need to do anything other than introduce the parameter class and change the method signature, but you would have to know about refactoring and the justification for making this change. To learn more about refactoring, read *Refactoring: Improving the Design of Existing Code*, by Martin Fowler, for more information on this subject.

Patterns and refactorings are not part of the UML, but they will help you to create better UML diagrams. Good designs don't have to have grammatically perfect UML, but patterns and refactorings will make your designs better.

Adding Supporting Documentation

Many modeling tools will take any documentation that you create and combine it with your diagrams and spit out high-quality—generally HyperText Markup Language (HTML)—cross-referenced and indexed model documentation. However, if you use a tool such as Excel, Word, Notepad, or something besides your UML tool to create your documentation, then you are defeating this feature of most tools.

I encourage you to convey as much meaning as possible with pictures. The simple reason is that pictures convey more information in a concise format than reams of text. If you need text, then try constraints and notes in the model, but keep these to a minimum. Finally, if you must add a lot of documentation, don't hold the programmers up while you write it. You will be lucky if the programmers even read your models—the truth hurts—let alone long-winded text. Unfortunately, many programmers are perfectly happy coding away whatever comes to mind or whatever they coded on their last project. Complicated models may end up being ignored models.

Generally, for posterity, I like to include a written architectural overview in a separate document that describes the system at a high level. Some people just can't or won't read models—think managers or even future programmers—but I create these documents near the end of the project when everyone else is busy debugging and testing.

Keep in mind that the UML and modeling are just one facet of software development. Modeling should help, not hinder, the overall process.

Validating Your Model

Many tools will validate models automatically. Unfortunately, every tool is different, and every tool seems to support different aspects of the UML. You can drive yourself crazy trying to remove bugs reported by validation tools from UML models. I wouldn't spend my time here. Period.

Your time will be better spent coding examples that show developers how to implement the model, teaching developers how to read the models, and walking through the models with the developers to see if they make sense and can be implemented. Generally, by the time you and the developers are happy with a particular diagram, the program has most of what your diagram describes coded anyway.

Finally, just as I wouldn't ship code with warnings or errors, I don't want to ship models with warnings or errors either. If model validation is reporting an error, then it usually means that I am using a feature inconsistently with the implementation of the UML my specific tool supports. Before I put a ribbon on a model and move on to something else, I will try to resolve discrepancies reported by validation tools. Historically, customers usually haven't been willing to pay for this effort, though.

Quiz

1. A model is only complete when it contains at least one of every kind of diagram.

   a. True

   b. False

2. Component diagrams are absolutely necessary.

   a. True

   b. False

3. I must pick either a top-down or a bottom-up approach to modeling but cannot combine techniques.

   a. True

   b. False

4. Specialization has been argued to yield productivity gains.

   a. True

   b. False

5. Design patterns are part of the UML specification.

   a. True

   b. False

6. Refactoring is not part of the UML specification.

   a. True

   b. False

7. Most experts agree that patterns and refactorings will improve the implementation of software.

   a. True

   b. False

8. The UML is a standard, and everyone agrees that it should be used.

   a. True

   b. False

9. Using a tool to validate models is essential.

   a. True

   b. False

10. All UML modeling tools are capable of effectively generating entire, complete applications.

   a. True

   b. False

Answers

1. b
2. b
3. b
4. a
5. b
6. a
7. a
8. b
9. b
10. b

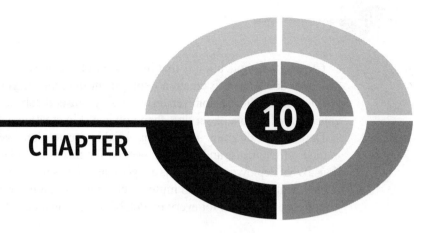

Visualizing Your Deployment Topology

Deployment topology simply means what your system will look like when you put it into use. You can diagram what your system will look like when deployed with a *deployment diagram*. Deployment diagrams will show the reader the logical elements, their physical locations, and how these elements communicate, as well as the number and variety of physical and logical elements.

Use deployment diagrams to show where your Web server is and whether you have more than one. Use deployment diagrams to show where you database server is and whether you have more than one and what the database server's relationship(s) is(are) to other elements. Deployment diagrams can show how these elements are connected, what protocols the elements are using to communicate, and what operating systems or physical devices, including computers and other devices, are present.

Clearly, the implication is that if you don't have most of these elements, then you probably don't need to create a deployment diagram. If you are creating a simple stand-alone application or even a simple single-user database application, a Web site, console application, or service, then you can skip creating a deployment diagram.

Deployment diagrams are not that hard to create, don't generally contain a large number of elements, and are only needed for medium- to large-complexity applications. What deployment diagrams are good at doing is visualizing the landscape of your deployment for systems with multiple elements. You are certainly welcome to create a deployment diagram for every model, but here is an area where I would economize.

Modeling Nodes

Nodes are three-dimensional boxes that represent physical devices that can but don't have to be computers or execution environments that can be computers, operating systems, or containing environments such as COM+, IIS, or an Apache server.

Physical devices commonly include computers, but they can include any physical device. Working on a project for Lucent Technologies years ago, I was writing software for hoteling phones—moving phone settings from phone to phone and controlling switching systems. In my deployment diagram, I showed computers, phones, and phone switches. More recently, I was working on a project for Pitney Bowes. I was writing a multinational shipping framework to support the concept of a universal carrier. Much of that framework used MSMQ—COM+ messaging queuing—so the deployment diagram reflected nodes that represented a COM+ execution environment.

The basic symbol for a node is a three-dimensional cube with the node name in the cube (Figure 10-1). If you wanted to model several nodes of the same type, then you could use a tag indicating the number of occurrences of that node, or you could add

Figure 10-1 A single-named node in a Unified Modeling Language (UML) deployment diagram.

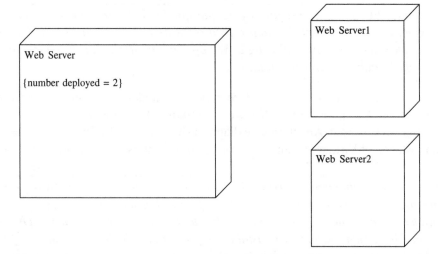

Figure 10-2   This diagram shows a tag indicating that there are two Web servers (left side) and two physical node Web servers on the right side.

multiple nodes to the diagram. Figure 10-2 shows how you might model a Web farm using the multiple-nodes tag on the left and multiple node symbols on the right.

In addition to using tags to indicate node multiplicity, we can use tags to indicate information about the node. For instance, in our Web server example, we could indicate that the nodes are all running IIS and Windows 2003 server. These additional tags are shown in Figure 10-3.

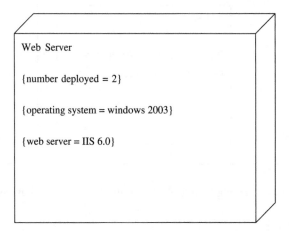

Figure 10-3   A partial deployment diagram showing multiple nodes and details about the operating system and version of Web server.

TIP *Virtual PC is a tool I use for having multiple logical computers on a single computer. It is an excellent way to test beta software or have a clean machine for local deployment, such as deploying a Web application to test for dependencies and proper setup and configuration.*

Finally, we can add one of two stereotypes to a node—«device» or «execution environment»—to indicate whether we are talking about a physical device or an executon environment. An alternative diagram showing a single Web server running in an instance of Virtual PC, an execution environment, is shown in Figure 10-4.

NOTE *An interesting and recurring challenge is that on long projects developers come and go. Generally, the result of a transition is that someone who has remained on the project has to spend an afternoon or a day helping the newcomer configure his or her machine. An installation project or a deployment diagram for the development environment might be as useful as a deployment diagram for a production system. (If you have a little extra time, try this out and see how it works.)*

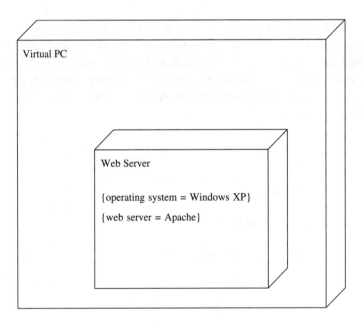

Figure 10-4   A node showing Virtual PC being used as an execution environment.

Showing Artifacts in Nodes

Artifacts are the things you are deploying. (If you are combining hardware and software development, then you might be deploying your own nodes too, but I am talking just about software.) Artifacts are modeled using the class symbol and an «artifact» stereotype. Artifacts can be .EXEs, .DLLs, HTML files, documents, .JAR files, assemblies, scripts, binary files, or anything else you deploy as part of your solution. Commonly, binary artifacts are components, and we can use a tag to specify which component an artifact represents. Figure 10-5 shows an artifact representing a .DLL, and Figure 10-6 shows how we would place that artifact in a node.

Traditionally, you might find some overlap between component diagrams and deployment diagrams. For example, if an artifact implements a component, you can show the component implemented as a tag, or you can add the component to the node showing the dependency between the artifact and the component. Figure 10-7 shows the component tag used to indicate that the shown artifact implements the "ExceptionManagement" component used, and Figure 10-8 shows the same thing using the more verbose dependency attached to a component symbol. (The «manifest» stereotype means that the artifact is a manifestation of the component.)

NOTE *Dependencies also can be used between artifacts to indicate that one artifact is dependent on a second. This supports the notion of references in .NET, uses in Delphi, and includes C++. For example, the "ExceptionManagement.dll" has a dependency on the "System.dll" (not shown) that contains the "EventLog" class in .NET.*

As an alternative to placing several nested class diagrams in a single node, the UML supports listing artifacts as text. For example, an ASP.NET-based Web site will contain a binary, several .ASPX files containing HTML and ASP, and possibly other documents or elements such as script. Using the class symbol for more than

```
<< artifact >>
motown-jobs.dll
```

Figure 10-5   An artifact representing a binary that is the executable supporting a Web site.

Web Server

{operating system = Windows 2003 Server}

{web server = IIS 6.0}

<<artifact>>
motown-jobs.dll

Figure 10-6 In deployment diagrams, artifacts are deployed to nodes, so we can show an artifact nested in a node.

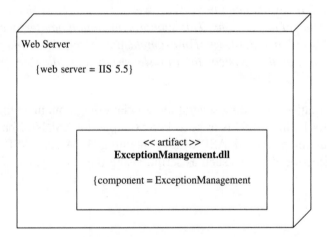

Web Server

{web server = IIS 5.5}

<< artifact >>
ExceptionManagement.dll

{component = ExceptionManagement

Figure 10-7 Specifying the component an artifact implements using a tag.

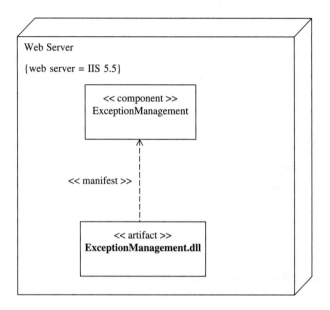

Figure 10-8   Specifying a component dependency using a component symbol.

a couple artifacts will result in the node being ridiculously large. List the artifacts as text if there are many of them. Figure 10-9 shows how we can list several artifacts in a single node.

If we were deploying the Web site's .DLL file in a Web farm, then each Web server node would be identical. In this instance, it would be easier to use the number-deployed tag in a single node rather than to repeat each node and diagram identical nodes.

Technically, you can add the combination of nodes, components, and artifacts that you need, and you can vary styles—text or symbols—based on how many elements a node has. However, keep in mind that if you have too many elements, then the diagram can become difficult to read. If you have a complicated deployment diagram, then try implementing a macro view with nodes, artifacts, and connectors and a micro view that expands on important aspects of the macro diagram. Show details in one or more micro views associated with the macro deployment diagram. For instance, consider showing the artifacts on the Web server, and if you want to

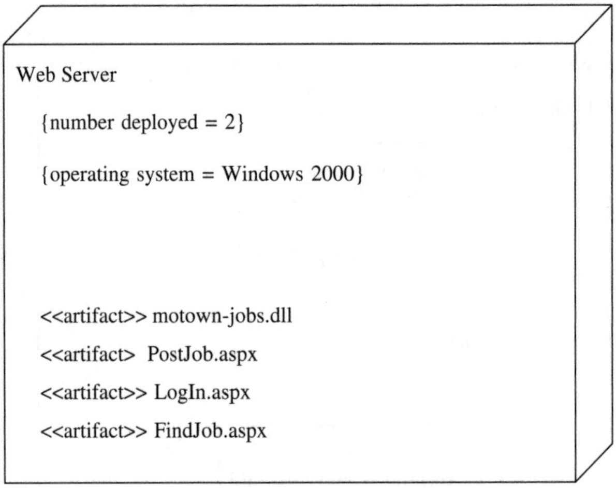

Figure 10-9   The UML supports using text to list artifacts, too.

expand on the relationship between the "ExceptionManagement.dll" artifact, the "ExceptionManagement" component, and the "EventLog," then create a separate view of this aspect of the system.

Adding Communication Paths

If you only have one node, then you don't need a deployment diagram. If you have more than one node, then you probably want a deployment diagram, and you will want to show how those nodes are connected and how they communicate.

There are two types of connectors used between nodes and artifacts in a deployment diagram. The association represents a communication path between nodes. The association shows the nodes that communicate, and a label on the association can be used to show the communications protocol between nodes. Additionally, an artifact can be drawn outside a node (a good approach for Visio, which doesn't support nesting artifacts in nodes) and attached to a node with a dependency and a «deploy» stereotype. The deploy dependency between an artifact and a node means the same thing as a nested artifact or a listed text artifact—that that kind of artifact is deployed on that kind of node.

Figure 10-10 demonstrates how we can externalize artifacts as an alternative way of showing where artifacts are deployed, and it also shows additional nodes and communication paths between those nodes. The communication paths are labeled if there is any interesting communication venue between nodes.

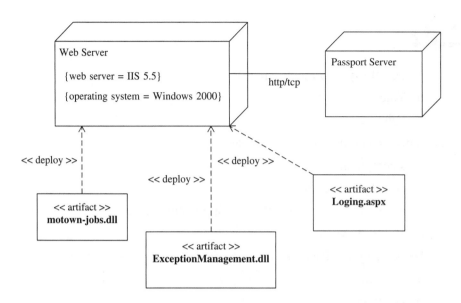

Figure 10-10   This figure shows that three artifacts are deployed on the Web server and that the Web server node communicates with a passport server via HTTP/TCP.

As is true with all diagrams, you can add notes, constraints, and documentation. You also can add as much or as little detail as you'd like. I have found that with any diagram, when you get past the point where the meaning can be understood at a glance, the diagram begins to lose its value to the reader. A good practice is to maintain some focus. If you want to show the entire system deployed, then show nodes and connections. If you want to elaborate on a single node, then create a new diagram and add detail for that node. Can you imagine how hard a single map of the world would be to read if it contained air navigation information as well as states, cities, towns, roads, railways, rivers, paths, trails, and topography? Think of UML diagrams as maps of your software with varying levels of detail: Different kinds of maps provide different kinds and levels of detail.

Now, having said all this, there has to be a way that as a modeler of a system you can articulate these steps in the process. Deployment diagrams are one facet to a *living application deployment* environment. Health monitoring and performance testing provide continuous feedback to the modeler that his or her hard work is working. I could go on at great length about this, but I feel that dropping a small hint might entice you to think more about the end product than just drawing pictures. Integrating those artifacts with real code and seeing the fruits of your labor realized all the time is quite gratifying. This is interesting, but not directly related to the UML. This has to do with incorporating "other" tools into a process.

Quiz

1. A node always represents a physical device.

    a. True

    b. False

2. A node can represent (pick all that apply)

    a. a computer.

    b. any physical device.

    c. an execution context such as an application server.

    d. all the above.

3. The stereotypes that apply to nodes can be (pick all that apply)

    a. «device».

    b. «component».

    c. «exceutionenvironment».

    d. «manifest».

4. Tags are used to add details to a node.

    a. True

    b. False

5. A database server is an example of a node.

    a. True

    b. False

6. Artifacts use which symbol?

    a. Package

    b. Class

    c. Activity

    d. Object

7. An artifact can be represented as text in a node, a class in a node, and with a realization connector and an external class symbol.

    a. True

    b. False

8. The connector and stereotype for an artifact shown outside a node is

   a. realization and manifest.

   b. dependency and deploy.

   c. association and deploy.

   d. dependency and manifest.

9. When an artifact is shown connected to a component, which stereotype applies?

   a. «deploy»

   b. «use»

   c. «manifest»

   d. «extends»

10. Which connector is used to show communication between nodes?

    a. Dependency

    b. Generalization

    c. Association

    d. Link

Answers

1. a
2. d
3. a and c
4. a
5. a
6. b
7. b
8. b
9. c
10. d

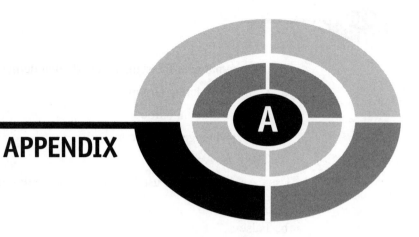

Final Exam

1. What does the acronym UML mean?

    a. Uniform Model Language

    b. Unified Modeling Language

    c. Unitarian Mock-Up Language

    d. Unified Molding Language

2. The UML is only used to model software.

    a. True

    b. False

3. What is the name of the process most closely associated with the UML?

    a. The modeling process

    b. The rational unified process

    c. Extreme programming

    d. Agile methods

4. What is the name of the standards body that defines the UML?

   a. Unified Modeling Group

   b. Object Modeling Group

   c. Object Management Group

   d. The Four Amigos

5. Use case diagrams are used to capture macro descriptions of a system.

   a. True

   b. False

6. Differentiate between sequence diagrams and collaboration diagrams (choose all that apply).

   a. Sequence diagrams are interaction diagrams; collaboration diagrams are not.

   b. Sequence diagrams represent a time ordering; collaboration diagrams represent classes and messages, but time ordering is not implied.

   c. Time order is indicating by numbering sequence diagrams.

   d. None of the above

7. A class diagram is a dynamic view of the classes in a system.

   a. True

   b. False

8. A good UML model will contain at least one of every kind of diagram.

   a. True

   b. False

9. What is the nickname of the group of scientists who are most notably associated with the UML?

   a. The Gang of Four

   b. The Three Musketeers

   c. The Three Amigos

   d. The Dynamic Duo

10. Sequence diagrams are good at showing the state of an object across many use cases.

    a. True

    b. False

11. What symbol represents an actor?

    a. A line

    b. A directed line

    c. A stick figure

    d. An oval containing text

12. An actor can be a person or something that acts on a system.

    a. True

    b. False

13. What symbol represents an association (pick the best answer)?

    a. A line.

    b. A line with a triangle pointing at the dependent element.

    c. A dashed line with an arrow pointing at the dependent element.

    d. A dashed line with an arrow pointing at the depended-on element.

14. Stereotypes are more common on

    a. actors.

    b. connectors.

    c. use cases.

    d. None of the above.

15. An inclusion relationship is used for modeling optional features reusing behavior modeled by another use case.

    a. True

    b. False

16. An extension relationship is used for modeling behavior captured by another use case.

    a. True

    b. False

17. Generalization is synonymous with

    a. polymorphism.

    b. aggregation.

    c. inheritance.

    d. interfaces.

18. Every capability of a system must be represented by a use case.

    a. True

    b. False

19. In an includes relationship, the arrow points at the

    a. base use case.

    b. inclusion use case.

20. It is important to implement the hard use cases first to mitigate risk early.

    a. True

    b. False

21. Synonyms for a transition are connector and flow.

    a. True

    b. False

22. In general, activity diagrams consist of (pick all that apply)

    a. nodes.

    b. transitions.

    c. decisions.

    d. edges.

23. Exceptions are not supported in activity diagrams.

    a. True

    b. False

24. A join and merge node use

    a. different symbols.

    b. identical symbols.

    c. either identical or differing symbols depending on context.

    d. All nodes symbols are the same.

25. Multiple flows entering an action node are not

    a. an implicit merge.

    b. an implicit join.

26. Flows wait at a merge until
    a. all flows have arrived.
    b. the first flow has arrived.
    c. you tell it to leave.
    d. It depends.

27. The swimlane metaphor is still in use.
    a. True
    b. False

28. Actions can exist in only one activity partition at the same time.
    a. True
    b. False

29. A join and fork node is represented by
    a. an oval.
    b. a circle.
    c. a rectangle.
    d. a diamond.

30. Activity diagrams are identical to flowcharts.
    a. True
    b. False

31. A collaboration diagram is an example of
    a. a sequence diagram.
    b. a class diagram.
    c. an activity diagram.
    d. an interaction diagram.

32. A collaboration diagram shows how an object's state evolves over many use cases.
    a. True
    b. False

33. Collaboration diagrams were renamed communication diagrams in the UML version 2.0.

    a. True

    b. False

34. Sequence diagrams cannot be used to model asynchronous and multithreaded behavior.

    a. True

    b. False

35. Interaction frames use a _____ (fill in the blank) to control when and which fragment of the frame to execute.

    a. merge

    b. join

    c. guard

    d. asynchronous message

36. The alt interaction frame is used to

    a. model optional behavior.

    b. model multithreaded behavior.

    c. model conditional logic.

    d. capture error conditions.

37. Sequence diagrams and communication diagrams show complementary views.

    a. True

    b. False

38. An activation symbol shows

    a. the lifetime of an object in a communication diagram.

    b. object creation.

    c. the lifetime of an object in a sequence diagram.

    d. object destruction.

39. A nested numbering scheme is valid UML used in

    a. sequence diagrams.

    b. activity diagrams.

    c. use cases.

    d. communication diagrams.

40. Sequence diagrams are perfect for modeling lines of code.

    a. True

    b. False

41. The same basic symbol is used for enumerations and interfaces.

    a. True

    b. False

42. When adding classes to a diagram, you should show fields and

    a. methods.

    b. fields only.

    c. properties.

    d. properties and methods.

43. A property can be modeled as a feature of a class and

    a. a subclass.

    b. an association class.

    c. a dependent class.

    d. an interface.

44. When modeling attributes, it is

    a. required that you model attribute methods.

    b. recommended that you not show attribute methods.

    c. recommended that you show the underlying fields for those attributes.

    d. None of the above

45. Simple types should be modeled as features and complex types as (pick the best one)

    a. features too.

    b. association classes.

    c. attributes.

    d. features or association classes.

46. A unidirectional association has an arrow at one end called the source. The other end is called the target.

    a. True

    b. False

47. An aggregation is most like

    a. inheritance.

    b. association.

    c. composition.

    d. generalization.

48. What is the most important difference between an aggregation and composition?

    a. Composition means that the whole, or composite, class will be responsible for creating and destroying the part or contained class.

    b. Aggregation means that the whole, aggregate class will be responsible for creating and destroying the part or contained class.

    c. Composition means that the whole, or composite, class is the only class that can have an instance of the part class at any given time.

    d. Aggregation means that the whole, or aggregate, class is the only class that can have an instance of the part class at any given time.

    e. a and c

    f. b and d

49. Realization means

    a. polymorphism.

    b. association.

    c. interface inheritance.

    d. composition.

50. A named association is modeled as a

    a. method.

    b. property.

    c. field and property.

    d. dependency.

51. A subclass has access to a superclass's protected members.

    a. True

    b. False

52. A child class may only have one parent class.

    a. True

    b. False

53. Which of the following statements is false?

    a. Generalization refers to subtypes.

    b. Classification refers to subtypes.

    c. Generalization refers to object instances.

    d. Classification refers to object instances.

    e. None of the above

54. Realization refers to

    a. class inheritance.

    b. interface inheritance.

    c. promoting the constituent members in a composite class.

    d. aggregation.

55. Multiple inheritance can be approximated through

    a. an association and the promotion of constituent properties.

    b. realization.

    c. composition and the promotion of constituent properties.

    d. aggregation and the promotion of constituent properties.

56. Dynamic classification—where an object's type changed at runtime—can be modeled using

    a. generalization.

    b. association.

    c. realization.

    d. composition.

57. An association class is not referred to as a linking class.

    a. True

    b. False

58. A parameter used to return a unique type is called

    a. a realization.

    b. an association qualifier.

    c. an association postcondition.

    d. directed association.

59. Pick the correct statements.

    a. A provided interface means that a class implements an interface.

    b. A required interface means that a class depends on an interface.

    c. A provided interface means that a class depends on an interface.

    d. A required interface means that a class implements an interface.

60. When a classifier symbol is underlined, it means that

    a. the symbol represents an object.

    b. the symbol represents an abstract class.

    c. the symbol represents an interface.

    d. the symbol is a derived value.

61. State charts (or state machine diagrams) are good for

    a. diagramming systems.

    b. diagramming objects and messages for a single use case.

    c. understanding a single use case.

    d. specifying the behavior of an object across several use cases.

62. State machines should not be used to explore graphical user interfaces (GUIs) and real-time controllers.

    a. True

    b. False

63. A junction is used to

    a. merge several incoming transitions to a single outgoing transition.

    b. split a single incoming transition into several outgoing transitions.

    c. Both a and b

    d. None of the above

64. History pseudostates are used to restore previous states.

    a. True

    b. False

65. A do activity executes

    a. over time and a regular activity executes immediately but can be interrupted.

    b. immediately and a regular activity executes over time but can be interrupted.

    c. over time and can be interrupted, and a regular activity executes immediately.

    d. over time and a regular activity executes immediately but cannot be interrupted.

66. Transitions are directed lines labeled with

    a. an optional trigger, an event, and an effect.

    b. a trigger, an optional event, and an effect.

    c. a trigger, an event, and an optional effect.

    d. a trigger, an event, and an effect optionally.

67. External transitions cause an enter and exit activity to be executed.

    a. True

    b. False

68. Self-transitions cause an enter and exit activity to be executed.

    a. True

    b. False

69. A composite orthogonal state

    a. is divided into regions, and only one region can be active at a time.

    b. is divided into regions, and only one substate can be active at a time.

    c. is divided into regions, and only one substate per region can be active at a time.

    d. is composed of a single region, and multiple substates can be active simultaneously.

70. A composite nonorthogonal state

    a. is comprised of regions, and only one region can be active at a time.

    b. is not divided into regions, and only one substate can be active at a time.

    c. is not divided into regions, and multiple substates can be active at a time.

    d. is divided into regions, and one substate per region can be active at a time.

71. Every model should contain at least one component diagram.

    a. True

    b. False

72. A bottom-up approach to component diagrams means that you

    a. define the components first and decompose those components into constituent parts.

    b. define the constituent parts and place the components on top of the constituent parts.

    c. Neither of the above

73. A bottom-up approach to design can be valuable because (pick all that apply)

    a. components aren't really needed.

    b. you get more traction solving domain problems first.

    c. building infrastructure is expensive and time-consuming.

    d. domain classes always can be organized into components at a later time.

74. Component symbols can be represented using a classifier with the «component» stereotype.

    a. True

    b. False

75. A required interface can be represented by a named half lollipop

    a. or a lollipop.

    b. or a dependency on a classifier with the «interface» stereotype.

    c. or by connecting to an interface with a dependency.

    d. only by using the half lollipop.

76. A provided interface is an interface that a component realizes.

    a. True

    b. False

77. A required interface can be represented by a named half lollipop and is equivalent to a dependency between a component and an interface.

    a. True

    b. False

78. Components may not contain nested components.

    a. True

    b. False

79. As a general rule, you only use components and component diagrams for systems with 100 or more domain classes.

    a. True, but this is a general guideline. Components can help you organize a solution and build reusable elements that can be sold separately.

    b. False, because building components is always cheaper in the long run.

80. For each domain class in a component-based architecture, you may need two to three supporting classes.

    a. True

    b. False

81. A model is only complete when it contains at least one of every kind of diagram.

    a. True

    b. False

82. Component diagrams are only needed for large systems.

    a. True

    b. False

83. I must pick either a top-down or a bottom-up approach to modeling but cannot combine techniques.

    a. True

    b. False

84. Specialization has been argued to yield productivity gains.

    a. True

    b. False

85. Design patterns are not part of the UML specification.

    a. True

    b. False

86. Refactoring is part of the UML specification.

    a. True

    b. False

87. Few experts agree that patterns and refactorings will improve the implementation of software.

    a. True

    b. False

88. The UML is a standard, and everyone agrees that it should be used.

    a. True

    b. False

89. Using a tool to validate models is essential.

    a. True

    b. False

90. All UML modeling tools are capable of effectively generating entire, complete applications.

    a. True

    b. False

91. A node always represents a physical device.

    a. True

    b. False

92. A node can represent (pick all that apply)

    a. a computer.

    b. any physical device.

    c. an execution context such as an application server.

    d. All the above

93. The stereotypes that apply to nodes are (pick all that apply)

    a. «device».

    b. «component».

    c. «executionenvironment».

    d. «manifest».

94. Tags are not used to add details to a node.

    a. True

    b. False

95. A database server is an example of a node.

    a. True

    b. False

96. Artifacts use which symbol?

    a. Package

    b. Class

    c. Activity

    d. Object

97. An artifact can be represented as text in a node, a class in a node, and with a realization connector and an external class symbol.

    a. True

    b. False

98. The connector and stereotype for an artifact shown outside a node is

    a. realization and manifest.

    b. dependency and deploy.

    c. association and deploy.

    d. dependency and manifest.

99. When an artifact is shown connected to a component, which stereotype applies?

    a. «deploy»

    b. «use»

    c. «manifest»

    d. «extends»

100. Which connector is used to show communication between nodes?

    a. Dependency

    b. Generalization

    c. Association

    d. Link

Answers

1. b	7. b	13. a
2. b	8. b	14. b
3. b	9. c	15. b
4. c	10. b	16. b
5. a	11. c	17. c
6. b	12. a	18. b

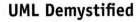
19. b	47. c	75. c
20. a	48. ?	76. a
21. b	49. c	77. a
22. a and d	50. c	78. b
23. b	51. a	79. a
24. a	52. b	80. b
25. a	53. b and c	81. b
26. a	54. b	82. b
27. a	55. c	83. b
28. b	56. b	84. a
29. c	57. b	85. a
30. b	58. b	86. b
31. d	59. a and b	87. b
32. b	60. a	88. b
33. a	61. d	89. b
34. b	62. b	90. b
35. c	63. c	91. b
36. c	64. a	92. d
37. b	65. c	93. a and c
38. c	66. d	94. b
39. d	67. a	95. a
40. b	68. a	96. b
41. a	69. c	97. b
42. a	70. b	98. b
43. b	71. b	99. c
44. b	72. b	100. c
45. d	73. b, c, and d	
46. a	74. a	

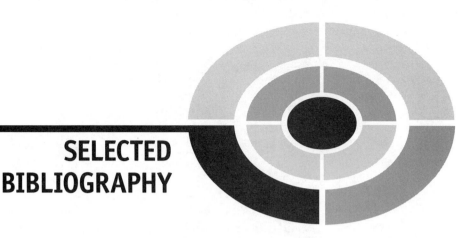

SELECTED BIBLIOGRAPHY

Ambler, Scott. *The Object Primer: Agile Model-Driven Development with UML 2.0*, 3d ed. New York: Wiley, 2004.

Booch, Grady. *Object Solutions*. Reading, MA: Addison-Wesley, 2005.

Booch, Grady, Ivar Jacobson, and James Rumbaugh. *The Unified Modeling Language*, 2d ed. Reading, MA: Addison-Wesley, 2005.

Eriksson, Hans-Erik, Magnus Penker, Brian Lyons, and David Fado. *UML 2 Toolkit*. Indianapolis: Wiley, 2004.

Fowler, Martin. *UML Distilled Third Edition: A Brief Guide to the Standard Object Modeling Language*. Reading, MA: Addison-Wesley, 2004.

Love, John F. *McDonald's: Behind the Arches*. New York: Bantam, 1995.

Övergaard, Gunnar, and Karen Palmkvist. *Use Cases: Patterns and Blueprints*. Reading, MA: Addison-Wesley, 2005.

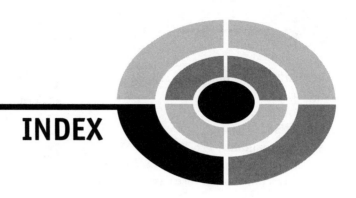

INDEX